Creating
Life-Like Animals
in Polymer Clay

Katherine Dewey

NORTH LIGHT BOOKS
CINCINNATI, OHIO
www.artistsnetwork.com

Dedication

*To the Kilroy man, my first and best teacher,
and others like him, artists and teachers
who share their knowledge for the love of their craft.*

Acknowledgments

To Maureen Carlson, who suggested I could; Greg Albert, who asked if I would; and Jennifer Long, who showed me how I should write this book: Thank you.

Thank you to Barbara McGuire of Accent Imports for providing samples of FIMO Soft and FIMO Stone.

Thank you to the people at Polyform Products for their extreme generosity.

Special thanks to photographer James Clay Walls of All Image Studios, San Marcos, Texas. He is a wizard with light.

Other fine North Light Books are available from your local bookstore, art supply store or direct from the publisher.

11 10   11 10 9

Library of Congress Cataloging-in-Publication Data
Dewey, Katherine
    Creating life-like animals in polymer clay / Katherine Dewey.
        p. cm.
    Includes index.
    ISBN-13: 978-0-89134-955-6 (alk. paper)
    ISBN-10: 0-89134-955-3 (alk. paper)
    1. Polymer clay craft. 2. Animal sculpture. I. Title.
TT297.D48 2000
731.4'2–dc21

                                            99-046378
                                            CIP

Editor: Jennifer Long
Production Coordinator: Kristen Heller
Cover design: Brian Roeth
Interior design: Wendy Dunning
Photography: James Clay Walls, All Image Studios, San Marcos, Texas

F+W PUBLICATIONS, INC.

About the Author

Katherine Dewey has been an award-winning, professional artist for twenty-seven years. One of the best-known figurative artists working in polymer clay, she is a regularly featured instructor for polymer clay associations such as the National Polymer Clay Guild, and a guest artist at polymer clay venues nationwide.

Born in Peoria, Illinois in 1944, Katherine was raised by parents who recognized her talent and introduced her to all of the arts. During her early college years she concentrated on the performing arts at the Pasadena Playhouse and Pasadena Junior College in Pasadena, California. When Katherine's family moved to Illinois, she began to explore the visual arts at Springfield College, the University of Illinois, Eastern Illinois University and Parkland College. She studied graphic design, sculpture and painting under several of the best artists in the region. Katherine also took many geology, history and biology courses to provide herself with a solid foundation for her work.

In 1968, Katherine struck out on her own as a freelance artist, designing and illustrating signs and brochures, rendering medical illustrations, and even constructing wildlife panoramas for the Illinois State Museum. Katherine has also put her artistic talent to work preparing taxidermy bird displays for the University of Florida, building architectural models, and designing costumes and masks for business and theater. She is also an aspiring novelist.

Married in 1969, Katherine and her husband spent the next twenty-four years traveling wherever his Air Force career took them. All the while, Katherine pursued and expanded her artistic horizons. When she and her family returned to Illinois in 1975, Katherine settled down to establish her business and simultaneously discovered polymer clay. This medium allowed Katherine to begin working three-dimensionally, without requiring access to specialized sculpting equipment and materials. Katherine soon earned a reputation as an accomplished polymer clay sculptor, attracting the attention of galleries and the press.

Today Katherine produces polymer clay sculptures for direct sale and through consignment to NanEtte Richardson Fine Arts, San Antonio, Texas; and Michael Mackie Fine Art, Dallas-Fort Worth, Texas. Katherine is a former executive board member of the Pacific Handcrafter Guild and a current member of the National Polymer Clay Guild, the San Marcos Art League and the Austin Writer's League.

Katherine and her husband Leo have two wonderful children, Kimberly and Padraic. Katherine lives in Maxwell, Texas.

Visit her Website at www.elvenwork.com.

Table of Contents

Introduction

There is nothing more satisfying than holding a lump of clay in your hands and pushing it into a simple shape. The satisfaction becomes delight as those same shapes evolve into complex, recognizable forms. This is a sensation I discovered long ago in a clay bank on the shores of Lake Michigan.

A secret place, a wonderful place, I spent one remarkable summer digging in that bank, pounding the streaky, gray clay until it was just right for modeling. I pushed it into simple shapes and put those shapes together.

Soon rabbits and mice, squirrels and raccoons and a deer with twiggy antlers lined the bank. Too soft to touch, too soft to move, my lumpy little animals remained on the bank where they baked hard in the summer sun, then melted with the first hard rain.

A few vanished, taken by a stranger who drew funny pictures in the clay, turning his footprints into long-nosed Kilroy faces and elephant ears. "Finders, keepers," he wrote. Beneath the words, underlining them, was a tiny spoon with its handle bent, the bowl beaten flat and smooth.

I set to work shaping the clay with my new tool, hoping the Kilroy man would leave more tools, that he would find my efforts worth sharing. Sometimes he did, and those were giddy moments. More often than not he left heartbreaking critiques. Once he destroyed one of my pieces utterly, replacing it with his own elegant creation, teaching me without words how to sculpt a horse.

Before summer's end I had acquired six tools, two books and a beginning knowledge of proportion. On the flyleaf of one of the books, his last gift to me, he wrote these words: "Thank you for sharing the delight. J.P."

I am still that child, working to please the Kilroy man. The clay I now use is very different, but the process is the same. This book is about that process. I cannot think of a better way of sharing the delight.

Katherine Dewey

CHAPTER ONE

A Polymer Clay Primer

There is nothing quite like polymer clay. Using this remarkable and colorful clay, artists can create intricately patterned jewelry, fabricate inlays and veneers, sculpt miniatures and dolls and more.

Polymer clay is versatile. With simple tools it can be sculpted and molded, then baked. The result can be painted, dyed, carved or sanded. More clay can be added and the piece modeled and baked again. Available at art and craft stores, hobby shops and super stores, polymer clay is the first clay of many amateurs and the clay of choice for many professionals.

Polymer clay is a manmade clay composed of very fine particles of polyvinyl chloride (PVC) suspended in an oily resin called a plasticiser. The plasticiser gives the clay flexibility. Pigments are added to the clay to give it color. Fillers, such as natural earth clays and chalks, give the clay its smooth texture. Baking polymer clay at the right temperature, between 200° and 275° F, fuses all of these elements. What was once a soft clay becomes a hard plastic.

When you first open a package of polymer clay, depending on the brand, it may feel very firm. Many polymer clays seem a bit hard at first, but once conditioned or kneaded they become surprisingly soft. That's because all polymer clays are sensitive to heat. The warmth of your hands, the warmth caused by friction and the warmth of a summer day can all affect polymer clay, making it softer. However, too much heat (above 100° F) over too long a time can partially bake the clay, making it firmer. Older clays may also become unusually firm because the fillers in the clay have absorbed some of the plasticiser.

There are many brands of polymer clay, each with its own qualities and array of colors. Colors may be opaque or translucent, iridescent or metallic, dusky or brilliant. The clays may be tacky or chalky. Some are very firm, others very soft. Some blend easily, while others do not. These are all qualities that different artists desire, qualities that suit the way they work, but what kind of clay is best for sculpting animals?

I like a strong, firm clay with a good "memory" and a quality I call the "smudge factor." A sculpture made of strong clay is less likely to

A clay better suited to modeling large figures, Cernit's extreme sensitivity to heat requires a bold but infrequent touch. This clay needs to rest and cool down frequently in order to hold its shape and texture. Cernit is a favorite of doll artists because of its excellent strength and translucent, porcelain finish, as seen in this white rabbit.

break after baking. Firm clay holds its shape during modeling. Clay with a good memory won't lose fine details, such as fur or feathers, while you are working. The "smudge factor" allows you to create a smooth, seamless sculpture, no matter how many pieces are added.

The Different Brands

Cernit

Cernit is a German clay manufactured by T+F GmbH. Initially waxy, firm and crumbly, Cernit becomes surprisingly soft and elastic as you work with it. Best for very large sculptures, this clay lacks the smudge factor and is extremely sensitive to heat—even body heat—making it a difficult clay for the beginning polymer clay sculptor, or for the sculptor acquainted with other modeling clays. Many artists like to blend Cernit with Super Sculpey, Sculpey III and FIMO Soft. The result is a more workable, but weaker, modeling clay.

The FIMO Family

FIMO, FIMO Soft, FIMO Stone and Mix Quick are all manufactured by Eberhard Faber. FIMO is a strong, firm clay with a slightly chalky feel. This clay may crumble fresh from the package, but a thorough kneading makes it very pliable. Sculptures made of this clay are very durable, but FIMO lacks the "smudge factor." It takes a bit of practice to blend a smooth seam without pushing the clay out of shape. If you use FIMO, use many light strokes rather than one or two heavier strokes to blend a smooth seam.

FIMO Soft is easy to condition and available in forty-eight colors. This slightly chalky clay has a good "smudge factor," but is very soft and has a poor memory. It requires a light touch. Blending FIMO Soft with original FIMO produces an excellent modeling clay.

Eberhard Faber also makes FIMO Stone and Mix Quick. FIMO Stone, a specialty clay with the look of stone, is available in six colors. Mix Quick, a clay softener, can be blended with overly firm or older clays to soften them.

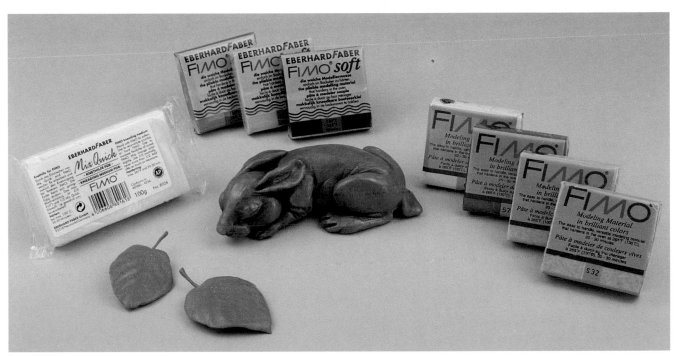

This faux jade rabbit and the two small leaves are made of FIMO Translucent tinted with FIMO Soft Green and FIMO Stone Jasper. Blending FIMO and FIMO Soft together produces a good modeling clay—soft enough for over-all shaping, yet firm enough for tiny details. A series of light, repetitive strokes is the key to blending FIMO, FIMO Soft or FIMO Stone.

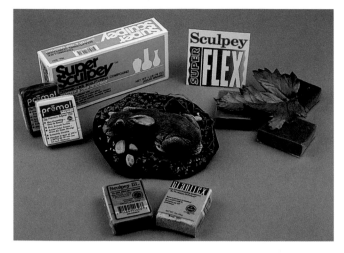

Polyform's products are well-represented in this painted rabbit sculpture, made of a blend of Premo and Super Sculpey. The base, made of Sculpey III, is dotted with rocks made of original white Sculpey and Granitex. The leaf, made of Sculpey Super Flex, is flexible and resists breakage. All of the Polyform clays are fairly soft and slightly tacky, but easy to model and blend. They vary in strength from original Sculpey, one of the weakest, to my favorite clay Premo, one of the strongest.

The Polyform Products

Polyform Products, an American company, manufactures several brands of polymer clay. Sculpey is the least expensive of all of the polymer clays, and the weakest. A very soft clay, Sculpey requires a light touch and bulky construction over a strong armature or inner skeleton. Available only in white, it has a tendency to scorch if overheated.

Super Sculpey is a strong, soft clay available only in beige. Its color, strength and excellent "smudge factor" make it a favorite of doll artists, and a favorite of mine. Many artists like to bake this clay at a lower temperature, but for a longer time to reduce scorching. This technique produces a beautiful finish, but a slightly weaker sculpture.

Sculpey III, available in thirty-two colors, is a very soft clay that requires a light touch. Sculptures made with Sculpey III need to have bulky components, a compact structure and a strong armature. This clay bakes to a matte finish, looking the least like plastic.

Premo Sculpey is the strongest of the Polyform clays. Designed as an all-purpose polymer clay with many applications, Premo is available in thirty-two colors. Because it is a soft and tacky clay, I use a technique called "leaching" (see page 13) to make this clay firmer and to reduce its tackiness.

Its strength and excellent smudge factor makes Premo my favorite polymer clay. Except for the white rabbit, the jade rabbit and the blue frog, all of the animals in this book were made with "leached" Premo.

Sculpey Super Flex is a soft clay that is still flexible after baking. A new product, it comes in eight basic colors. Artists are just beginning to explore its potential.

Polyform also makes Granitex, Sculpey Diluent and Liquid Sculpey. Granitex is a specialty clay available in eight pastel colors. Tinted fibers added to the clay give it a granite-like appearance. However, blending Granitex with a colored clay such as Premo softens the textured look of the clay.

Sculpey Diluent, a liquid used to soften very firm clay, can also be used to strengthen the bond between baked and unbaked clays.

Liquid Sculpey is a liquid polymer used in silicone injection molds. It's also an excellent polymer glue, useful for bonding baked clay components together. Artists often tint Liquid Sculpey with dry pigments to create their own polymer-based paints.

SAFETY TIPS

- Before you start any project with polymer clay, stop and read the label. Just as each clay has different characteristics, each clay has different instructions for use. Baking temperatures vary from brand to brand and sometimes from color to color.
- While you're reading that label, look for the AP Nontoxic Seal. Make sure the clay meets the Art & Creative Materials Institute's safety standards. Polymer clay is not a toy. It's a creative medium. Treat it as one.
- When a sculpture is in the oven, use the ventilator fan. Polymer clay releases fumes when baking. The odor, while not altogether unpleasant, may bother some.
- When baking clay, use an accurate oven thermometer. Baking above 360° F will burn the clay. The fumes released by burning clay are not only irritating, they're hazardous.
- The AP Nontoxic Seal does not mean polymer clay is safe to eat; it means the clay is nontoxic if used properly. Don't use it to create food containers; resins in baked polymer clay are not fully inert and may leach into the food.
- For the same reason, if you work at the kitchen table, protect it from the clay. It might be old and battered, but it's also where you prepare food.
- If you use kitchen utensils as tools, don't return them to the kitchen. Any tools used for polymer clay must be relegated to clay work only. You're an artist now, and that garlic press, rolling pin or baking dish are now artist's tools.
- Keep your work area clean. It will free your mind so the ideas can flow and will protect your clay from dust and fibers that can contaminate it. Keeping your work area clean means putting your clay away when you're finished—away from the kids, the dog, the cat, the iguana …
- When you put that clay away in a sealed container, store it with the label. There's valuable information on that label.
- If your kids want to play with the clay, play with them, but make sure they treat the clay as you do, as a creative medium. Naturally, everyone must wash their hands when they're finished.

CHAPTER TWO

Tools of the Trade

F or the modeler, the best tools for the job are often your hands. Sometimes, however, you need a little tool—or a big one.

Oven

One of the most essential tools for working with polymer clay is an oven. It may be a standard gas or electric oven or a smaller convection or toaster oven. Never use a microwave. In a microwave oven, resins in the clay will boil and cause the clay to explode or ignite.

Many artists dedicate a smaller convection or toaster oven strictly for polymer clay use. Because my sculptures are often too large for these countertop ovens, I use my kitchen oven and clean it regularly. Most sculptures in this book are too large to be safely baked in a countertop oven.

Baking Surfaces

The right baking surface is essential. Glass baking pans are best. They conduct heat at a slower rate than metal, allowing the clay to heat and cure more evenly. If you use a metal baking pan, layer it with baking parchment to reduce scorching.

A ceramic tile and a glass baking dish are the only baking surfaces I use. Small trays made of card stock help keep tiny components like eyeballs in place. Cotton batting or folded paper towels provide a cushioned surface that won't mar the texture of an animal when it's laying down.

Work Surfaces

Your work surface should be smooth and impervious to clay. Oils from the clay may ruin a fine wood table. I use a variety of work surfaces: a smooth ceramic floor tile, a sheet of tempered display glass, a self-healing craft mat and a sheet of graph paper. The tile and glass are resistant to scratches, impervious to the clay and can serve double duty as baking surfaces. The craft mat is marked with a grid, making it a

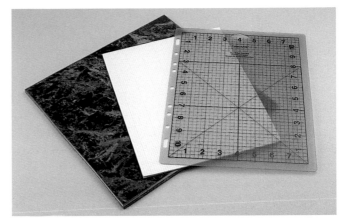

Shown here are a smooth, ceramic floor tile, a self-healing craft mat and a sheet of graph paper. Inexpensive and portable, these are the surfaces I use to protect my workbench from knife cuts and clay residue.

useful tool for cutting and measuring the clay. The graph paper can be used in the same way, and it's also very cheap, portable and absorbs plasticiser from very soft clay, making the clay firmer as I work.

Modeling Tools

To make a smooth seam in a tight spot or to create detail in your sculptures, you need tools smaller than your fingers.

Modeling tools made for natural earth clays and plasticine (a natural earth clay suspended in nondrying oil) all work well with polymer clay. Tools made for jewelers who work in wax are also good for the polymer clay sculptor. Dental instruments—all those picks, scrapers and scalers that are a pain for the patient—are a joy for the small-scale sculptor. I especially like the Woodson 3 Plastic Filling

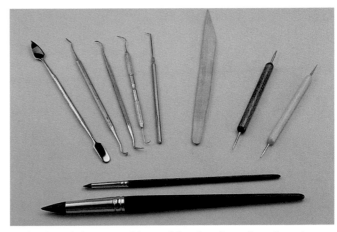

Steel tools made for wax modeling and dental work are shown here alongside wood-handled ceramic tools. In the foreground are soft, rubber-tipped Clay Shapers made by Foresline and Star.

Instrument. This small spatula has many modeling uses.

My favorite tools are those I made myself, tools that evolved out of a particular need as I evolved as a sculptor. Made of knitting, sewing and tapestry needles, my favorite tools serve as tiny fingers, allowing me to draw furry lines and roll smooth seams. You'll need these tools to create the animals in this book.

Making Your Own Tools

The no. 2 and no. 7 double-ended aluminum knitting needles listed at right are just the right size, ready for modeling. Throughout this book you'll find them referred to as the small (no. 2) and medium (no. 7) knitting needles.

You'll also need a large knitting needle, a no. 11 or 11½. Rather than purchase the shorter, double-ended type, buy a longer, single-ended needle. You'll use at least 6" (15.2cm) measured from the point as your large knitting needle tool, but the rest you'll use to make strong handles for your fine modeling tools.

Making Handles for Your Fine Modeling Tools

You will need three handles for your fine modeling tools. Aluminum knitting needles size 10 and larger are hollow and make great handles. Cutting the needles into tubes is easily done with a tube cutter or a strong, straight blade. When you cut them, make sure they're long enough for comfort; 3" to 5" (7.6cm to 12.7cm) should do just fine.

Fill each handle with thoroughly kneaded polymer clay by rolling the clay into a thin rod and feeding it into the tube. Feed small sections of the rod of clay at a time, stopping to tamp it down with a

dowel rod or paintbrush handle. When the tubes are packed with clay, you're ready to insert the needles halfway into the clay, eye first.

The fine needle tool is a medium sewing needle inserted into a handle, point out. Because it is sharp, it should be a single-ended tool.

To make the blunt needle tool, insert a no. 16 tapestry needle, point out, into a handle. Insert a no. 20 tapestry needle, point out, into the other end.

Your third tool is a landscape tool. At one end insert a small drill bit. In the other end insert a no. 20 tapestry needle into the clay, point first, then use a wire cutter to snap the eye in half, creating a fork.

Make certain the clay is well packed around each of the tips. Bake your tools in a glass pan for twenty minutes at 275° F.

SUPPLIES
- Stiff brass rod
- Double-ended aluminum knitting needles, no. 2 and no. 7
- One pair of no.11 or no. 11½ aluminum knitting needles
- Medium sewing needle
- Two no. 20 tapestry needles
- One no. 16 tapestry needle

Tools for Making Tools
- Dowel rod or small paintbrush
- Wire cutters
- Small drill bit
- Strong, sharp blade (a glass scraper or knife)

Polymer Clay
- Two ounces (56.7g) of any color strong polymer clay (Premo, FIMO or FIMO Soft)

To cut hollow aluminum knitting needles (size 10 and larger) down to a practical size, use a tube cutter or a strong, sharp blade. For the latter technique, which I learned from designer and metalsmith Christopher Hentz, place the needle on a cutting board with the head just off the edge of the board; this insures it rolls smoothly. Hold the blade perpendicular to the knitting needle. Use the pressure of the blade to roll the knitting needle back and forth, creating a groove around the shaft. When the blade begins to stick, stop cutting and snap the tube in half. A standard no. 11 knitting needle will make four strong handles.

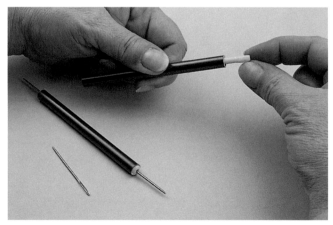

Feed a rod of kneaded polymer clay into the tube and use a dowel rod or the handle of a paintbrush to pack it in tightly. When the tube is full, insert the smaller needle into the clay. Your tools may be single- or double-ended.

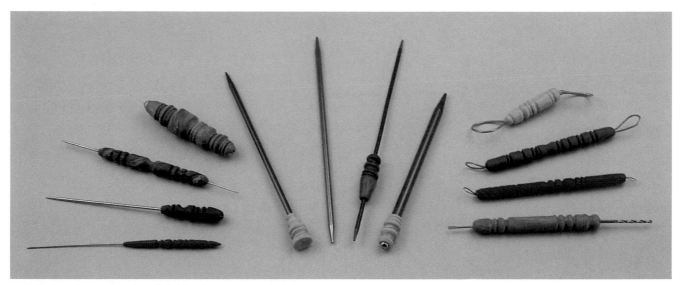

Look closely at these tools and you'll find familiar objects. On the left are a sewing needle, a pair of tapestry needles set into one handle, and two very long weaving needles. In the center are knitting needles, some cut down to a more practical size and fitted with polymer clay handles. On the right are clay rakes, loops made of stiff brass rods that scrape clay smooth or impress curved lines. The blue-handled tool in the right front is my landscape tool, with a small drill bit set in one end and a "grass fork" set in the other end. The fork—a needle eye cut in half—is useful for planting grass in soft, un-baked clay, while the drill makes holes in hard, baked clay.

Making Clay Rakes

Less important, but equally simple to make, are clay rakes. These loops, made by bending a stiff brass rod around different-sized dowel rods, serve as scrapers to "rake" the clay smooth. Their round shape also impresses curved lines in the clay, useful for shaping a very round eyelid.

If you wish to make a set of rakes, use only brass rods, not wire. Brass wire is too soft, and other metals, especially aluminum, leave a dark residue on the clay.

Brass rods (mine are manufactured by K & S Engineering) are available at hobby shops that cater to the finescale modeler.

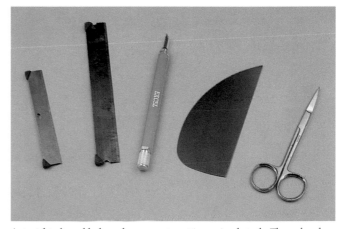

A straight, sharp blade makes accurate cutting a simple task. The red, polymer clay handles on the dull edges of two of these blades enable me to pick up very thin and dangerously sharp blades without cutting my fingers. The unusual wing-shaped blade is a metal potter's rib, sharp enough to cut the clay, yet dull enough for the young modeler. For cutting paper patterns and armatures, a precision craft knife or a small pair of scissors will do the job.

Tools for Cutting

Accurate modeling depends on using the right amount of clay for the job. This means measuring and cutting the clay using a ruler or template and a straight, sharp blade. The tissue blade (made for laboratory work), Donna Kato's Nu-blade (made for cutting polymer clay) and a glass scraper blade all have long, straight, very sharp blades that will easily cut through the clay. These blades should be used with caution.

Less sharp, but equal to the task, is the metal potter's rib. Made for forming pots on the wheel, the rib has a straight edge and is a good choice for children.

For sharp cuts in tight spots, use a craft knife with a razor sharp blade. A good pair of scissors, such as those used by decoupage artists, will often do the same job. These scissors are another good choice for the young sculptor.

Tools for Rolling

For years I used a rolling pin to roll sheets of clay. The sheets were never truly uniform and the job was never fun. Now I use a pasta machine. It's a lifesaver! This device has never seen a noodle, but it has saved me hours of work. It rolls truly uniform sheets of clay in varying thicknesses ranging from paper thin to ⅛" (0.3cm).

Tools for Strength

Within most of the sculptures in this book is an armature, a support that makes it stronger. To make these armatures, you'll need needle nose pliers, wire cutters, a small hammer and a ruler.

Tools for Painting

Animals are colorful creatures with spots and stripes, wet noses and shiny eyes. I create these realistic details with acrylic paint. Oil paints, alkyds and model paints react badly with polymer clay—the surface remains tacky. Watercolors and tempera tend to bleed into the fillers in the clay, an effect that occurs most often with FIMO.

Acrylics dry rapidly, are relatively inexpensive and readily available. If mistakes are made, the sculpture can be scrubbed clean. Craft paints are more opaque and tend to cover more quickly than artist pigments, but these same craft paints tend to be less durable after drying.

Artist's pigments, available in the tube or jar, are more transparent and produce a slight sheen after drying, but have greater durability.

Blending the two types of paints together combines the best qualities of both—a slight matte finish with greater durability. I recommend acrylics and have used them to paint the animals in this book.

Apply these paints with good brushes. China bristle brushes are an excellent and inexpensive tool for dry brushing, a painting technique that enhances texture. You'll also need a no. 5 or no. 6 round or filbert. There are synthetic brushes made to withstand the abrasive effects of acrylic paints, but I prefer a natural bristle such as sable. With the right care, your brushes will last a long time. A no. 00 or no. 000 detail or liner brush will help you create the final details.

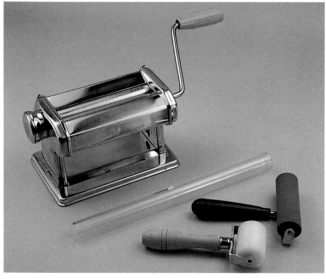

While the pasta machine rolls uniform sheets of clay and is my roller of choice, sometimes it's more than I need. Both a printer's brayer and a wallpaper seam roller are good for rolling small, thick or thin sheets, while the Lucite rod rolls much wider sheets of clay.

Whether you use crafter's or artist's pigments, in a tube or in a jar, acrylic paints are a proven paint for polymer clay. Craft paints such as Plaid's FolkArt, DecoArt Americana and Delta Ceramcoat are fairly opaque and have a matte finish.

Artist colors such as Liquitex, Winsor & Newton Galleria and Grumbacher Hyplar are more transparent and have a slight sheen.

Flecto Varathane Elite Diamond Finish, an acrylic varnish made for wood finishing, is the best varnish I've found for polymer clay. Other varnishes, even acrylic varnishes, may react with the clay and take weeks, even months, to fully dry.

CHAPTER THREE
Mastering the Basics

From modeling simple shapes to understanding proportion, this chapter is about the basics—the practical steps that create a good polymer clay sculpture. This process begins with conditioning the clay.

The Need to be Kneaded

Soft or firm, all polymer clays require conditioning or kneading. With firm clays, the benefits become immediately obvious as a hard crumbling lump suddenly becomes workable. With soft clays, the benefits become obvious only if the clay is stressed after baking—conditioned clay is stronger clay.

Making Soft Clay Firmer

Soft clays require a delicate touch. For my techniques, I recommend a firm clay. Although I use Premo, which is initially a very soft clay, I make it firmer by removing some of the plasticiser. This process, called "leaching" or "wicking," takes a day or two, but the resulting clay is ideal for sculpting. It's soft enough for overall shaping, yet firm enough to hold fine details such as fur or feathers.

Only the soft, smudgeable, strong clays improve with wicking. Super Sculpey and Premo are two brands that do. Sculpey III and FIMO Soft both become more workable and easier to control when leached, but removing plasticiser also removes some of the clay's flexibility. These two clays are fairly brittle after baking and leaching makes them more brittle. Two other clays that don't benefit from wicking are FIMO and Cernit.

Knead, then roll the clay in your hands to form a long cylinder. Fold and twist, then roll another cylinder. Continue folding, twisting and rolling for about five minutes or until the clay is uniformly pliable. If the clay is one of the firmer brands, or if it's old, break or chop it into small pieces, then work the pieces together before you begin conditioning.

A small food chopper can help condition clay. To protect the machine's motor, process small chunks of clay for one minute intervals. As the blades break up the clay, friction warms and softens it. When clumps form, the clay is ready for kneading.

Use a pasta machine to condition the softer clays. Flatten the clay until it's a little thicker than ⅛" (0.3 cm), then run it through the rollers at the largest setting. Fold in half and run it through the machine again, always feeding it fold first. Repeat the process on the same setting ten to fifteen times.

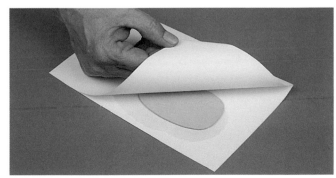

To make a soft clay firmer, condition it, then roll it into thin sheets. Sandwich the clay between clean sheets of paper and place a weight on top. Let it rest for a day. The paper will draw plasticiser from the clay. Recondition the clay and model a few simple shapes to determine if it feels right for you. Wick again if you want a firmer clay.

A Method for Modeling

Understanding how basic shapes fit together to form a complex animal will make the process of modeling easier to master. When you finish sculpting the animals in this book, you will want to create other animals, creatures of your own design, sculpted from your own patterns. It begins here, with a very basic understanding of form and proportion.

An animal's distinctive form is a combination of a few simple shapes. In each project in chapter four you'll find pattern guides that illustrate how the very basic shapes in an animal's head and body combine to produce that animal.

Many animals have shapes in common; it is the variations in the size and placement of these shapes that distinguish one species from another. These variations are the animal's proportions. How much clay you use to sculpt an animal's distinctive features depends on its proportions. Using the right amount of clay ensures that the head isn't too large or small for the body, that the limbs are equal in size, that all of the basic shapes fit together. Using the right amount of clay means measuring the clay.

Measuring the Clay

How accurately you measure the clay is as important as the shapes you model and combine. This book illustrates two methods for measuring the clay: the block method and the rod method.

The Block Method

Both methods depend on a measuring gauge called the base unit, a ball of clay with a specific diameter. Each animal has its own base unit (found in the animal's pattern guide). With each project you'll find a photograph and instructions for measuring the clay using the block method. The photo shows you the color or colors of the clay, how much clay you'll need for that sculpture and how to divide the clay into the base unit using a ruler to measure and a straight blade to cut the block. The block method uses two-ounce (56.7g) blocks of Premo.

The Rod Method

If you purchase your clay in one pound (.45kg) bricks, or use a brand other than Premo, you'll need to use the rod method to measure the clay. As precise as cutting the clay from the block, the rod method also depends on the base unit.

Beside the base unit diagram of each animal, you'll find a straight line. This line is ⅔ of the diameter of the base unit. If you roll a rod of clay the same diameter as the base unit, cut the rod into slices the length of the line (⅔ of the diameter), then roll each slice into a ball, those balls will have the same diameter as the rod, the same diameter as the base unit and the same diameter as if you cut the clay using the block method.

There's a similar line next to each eyeball diagram. Again, use a straight blade to cut the rod and use a divider, compass, caliper or sewing gauge set to the ⅔ measurement to mark the rod.

With a little practice, you'll have no trouble cutting the base unit balls into smaller units for shaping muzzles and mouths, bellies and backs.

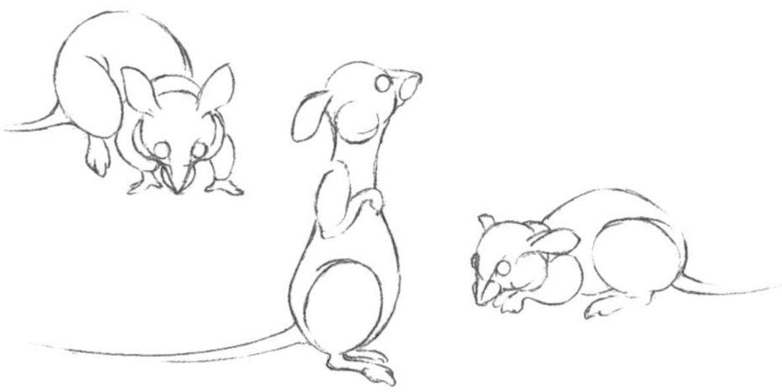

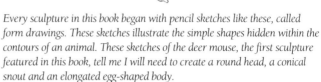

Every sculpture in this book began with pencil sketches like these, called form drawings. These sketches illustrate the simple shapes hidden within the contours of an animal. These sketches of the deer mouse, the first sculpture featured in this book, tell me I will need to create a round head, a conical snout and an elongated egg-shaped body.

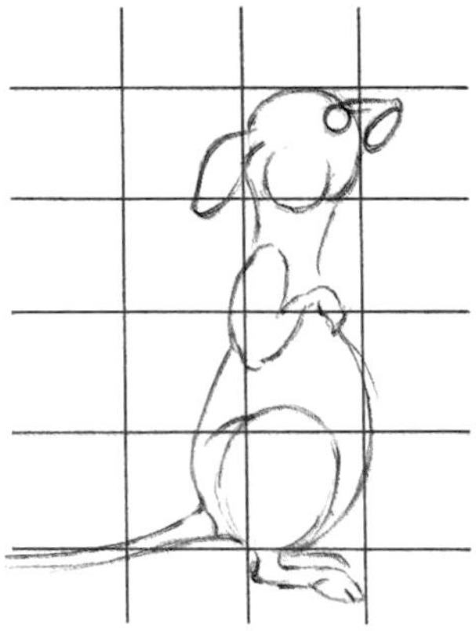

A superimposed grid provides a clue to the mouse's proportions, the relative size of one body part to another. The circle shape of the mouse's head is the simplest shape in this sculpture, so I will use it as the base unit.

The grid tells me the mouse's body is roughly four times larger than the circle shape of his head, or four times the base unit. The snout is ¼ the size of the head circle, or ¼ of the base unit. If I use these proportions to measure the clay, one ball of clay will form the mouse's round head and ¼ of a ball will shape his snout. Four balls of clay, each the same diameter as the original ball, will build his egg-shaped body. Every sculpture in this book has its own base unit.

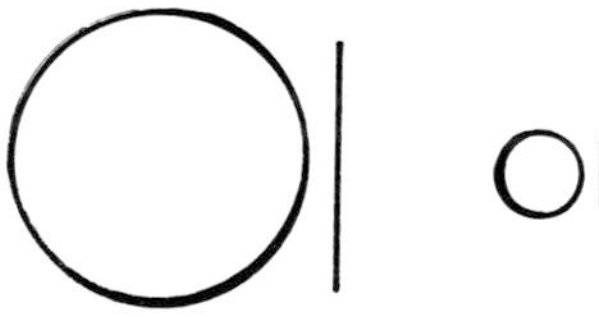

Circles like this appear in each project. They illustrate the diameters of the base unit and the eyeball. The lines next to them represent ⅔ the diameters. You'll use both the diameter and the line if you prefer to measure your clay using the rod method.

To use the rod method, roll a rod of conditioned and leached clay until it is the same diameter as the base unit or eyeball. A sewing gauge is an inexpensive device for marking the rod. Set the gauge to match the line drawn beneath the base unit and press it against the rod, leaving two marks in the clay. Continue marking the rod by pressing each mark into the previous mark. Cut the rod at each of the marks. Each slice will produce a ball of clay the same diameter as the rod and the base unit.

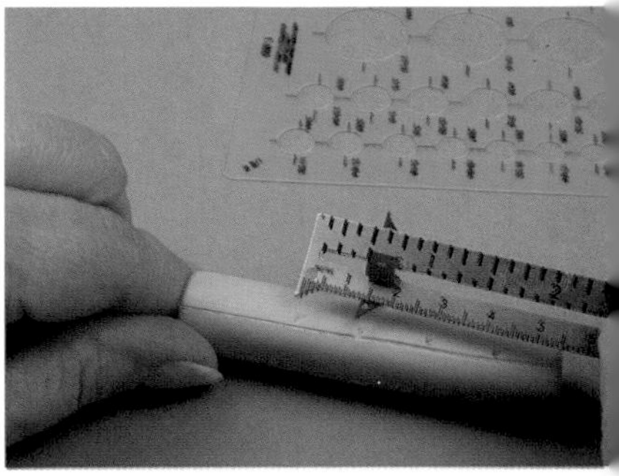

Mastering the Basic Shapes

The sphere or ball, the oval or egg shape and the cylinder or rod are all very simple, basic shapes. Their simplicity makes them versatile, powerful. Combined according to a pattern, they can produce very complex animal forms.

Balls of clay become eyeballs or the skeletal beginnings of an animal's head. Flattened balls, or disks, can build up a jaw line or add fat to an animal's belly or rump. Egg shapes fulfill a variety of modeling needs from shaping heads and bodies to limbs. Flattened eggs add additional shape and definition to a profile or limb. Rods of clay become limbs, muscles or folds in the skin. Flattened rods, or strips of clay, can enhance the shape of an animal in subtle, but noticeable, ways. These shapes are essential components of the practical modeling method.

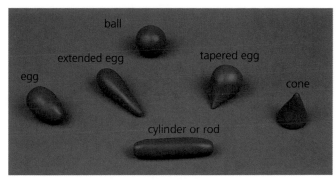

These basic shapes, similar to those found in the form drawings, are fundamental to every animal sculpture.

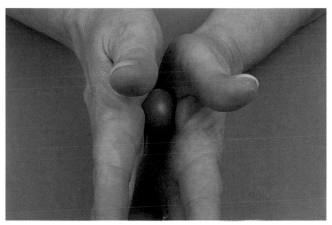

BALL

Even the smallest shapes begin as a smooth, round ball. The key to rolling a well-rounded ball lies in your hands, in the curvature of your palms and the pressure you exert. Too much pressure will result in a bi-cone, a shape similar to a toy top. If that happens, use your fingers to give it a rounder shape, then re-roll gently.

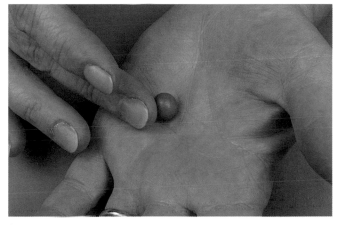

SMALL BALL

Use your finger to roll smaller balls in the hollow of your hand.

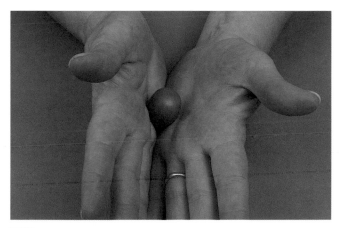

EGG

*To form an egg, hold your palms together in a **V** shape and roll the ball back and forth two or three times.*

SMALL EGG

Shape a small egg by rolling the ball back and forth with your finger in the hollow of your palm.

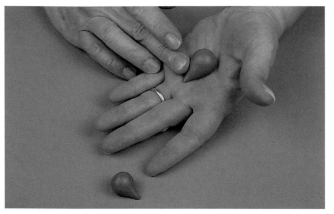

TAPERED EGG

Many animal heads use this sharply tapered egg. Roll an egg back and forth with your finger in the hollow of your palm. Use you thumb and fingers to caress the tip to a point.

EXTENDED EGG

Many limbs begin as an extended egg. The longer you roll the egg back and forth, the more elongated it becomes.

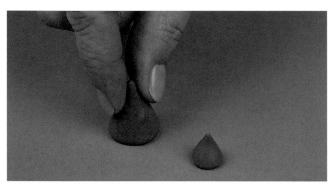

CONE

Press a tapered egg against a flat surface to form a cone. Reshape the tip with your fingers if it becomes pinched and misshapen.

ROD

Shape cylinders by rolling a ball of clay back and forth on a flat surface. Exert even pressure as you move your hands apart. Practice this technique; you'll use it to measure the clay.

APPLIQUÉS

Appliqués are flattened forms of the basic shapes. Balls become disks and are used to round out cheeks. Flattened eggs and extended egg shapes become animal thighs or define a muzzle. Cylinders become strips or ovals, depending on the width and length of the original shape. Flatten small appliqués by gently pressing them between your thumb and finger. Exert even pressure so that the appliqué has an even thickness, usually ³⁄₁₆" (0.5cm). Flatten larger appliqués by pressing them between the palms of your hands, or use your fingers and gently press down on the work surface.

ASSEMBLY TECHNIQUES

How you blend the seams is just as important as the shapes themselves. Always:

• Follow the step-by-step instructions. Don't attach pieces out of order or all at once.

• Shape the appliqué—the piece you're adding—just before you attach it. The seams will blend more easily if the appliqué is warm and the base piece is cool.

• Work the clay from the added piece or appliqué onto the base piece.

• Blend the seams of one appliqué at a time, even if they are matching pairs.

Using Tools to Model, Blend and Texture

Knitting and sewing needles are powerful modeling tools. With these simple tools you can press, shape and stroke the clay in ways and in places your hands cannot. Use the shaft of a knitting needle to blend seams. Press a sewing needle into the clay to define paws. The point of a needle can pierce the clay or create texture.

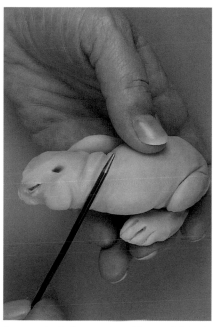

Pivoting the shaft across this rabbit's neck helped to create folds in his skin. You can also use this technique to suggest muscle and bone.

Creating Texture

Realistic animal sculptures have more than form and proportion. They're furry or feathery, warty or scaly. They have texture. The techniques for creating realistic furry textures are as simple and familiar as using a pencil. Stroking the clay with a knitting or tapestry needle can yield remarkable results.

Use the tapered tip of a knitting needle as a roller to blend seams in tight spaces.

To create a sleek, furry texture, use a tapestry needle and mark long, closely-spaced lines in the clay. Laying the shaft of the needle on the clay and gently pulling will give you the control you want, especially if the clay is very soft.

The thickly-furred texture of this bear called for a combination of techniques and tools. I marked overlapping rows of short, closely-spaced strokes on most of his body and head with the point of a large knitting needle. Varying the pressure gave the fur a dense and tufted appearance. The shorter fur of his muzzle called for gentler strokes with a finer tool, the tapestry needle.

TIP

When you're creating texture, especially fine texture, use a single light source set at a 45°angle. Let it shine over your left shoulder if you're right-handed and vice versa. Each strand of fur you draw will cast a fine shadow, allowing you to see every detail and smudge.

Building Armatures

Inside most animals is a source of inner strength: a skeleton. Animal sculptures, even small ones, sometimes need a bone or two. Stiff brass bones keep limbs from buckling and support heavy heads. Heavy paper replaces the cartilage in ears. Tightly packed aluminum foil can fill a fat belly, reducing the amount of clay, the weight of the sculpture and adding strength. Using armatures will make your sculptures stronger, lighter, better.

The polar bear shown on the previous page is filled with foil; a round foil core in his head, an egg-shaped core filling his body. His legs are the thickest clay components at ½" (1.3cm). Because of the armature, it took less than an hour to bake the bear. The little rabbit on the previous page, modeled entirely of clay, required more than two hours in the oven and used more clay.

Though it takes a little more effort to produce a well-shaped foil core, the savings in time and clay are well worth it.

Brass rods, my favorite "bones," make for strong limbs and stiff spines. Beading wire replaces tiny bones. Card stock replaces the cartilage in thin ears. Balls and eggs of densely packed aluminum foil fill bodies. Cyanoacrylate glues, such as Super Glue or Crazy Glue, strengthen card stock, making it stronger. Sobo, Gem Tac and Aleene's Tacky Glue are vinyl glues that adhere clay to paper and wire.

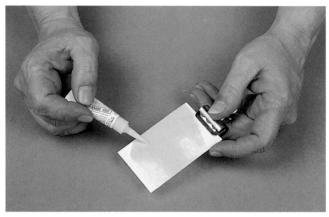

SIZING CARD STOCK
For stiffer, stronger card stock armatures, size the card with a cyanoacrylic glue (Super Glue). Hold the card with a bulldog clip rather than your fingers while you work since these glues bond instantly with skin. Apply small drops at a time, using the applicator to spread the glue as it penetrates the paper. Cyanoacrylic glues can release irritating vapors. Work slowly and carefully in a well-ventilated area. Let dry fifteen minutes or more.

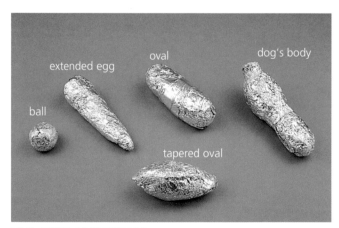

FOIL CORE ARMATURES
These are the types of foil cores used to support the animals in this book. Though each is a different shape, all use similar construction techniques. Measuring the foil sheets insures that the finished foil core will be the right size.

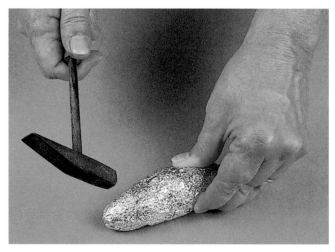

A small, lightweight hammer is a good tool for refining the shape of foil cores.

COVERING FOIL CORES—THE PLASTER LAYER
Pack small pieces of clay into the crevices until the core has a uniform shape. Continue applying small pieces of clay, building up a thin coating of clay. This is called the plaster layer. The foil that shines through will be covered in the next step.

THE WRAPPING LAYER
Roll an ⅛" (0.3cm) thick sheet of clay large enough to fold around the core. It should have the same overall outline of the core. Blend the seams, then rub the clay-covered core gently using your fingers or the palms of your hand.

Baking Techniques

How long you bake a sculpture is as important as the temperature at which you bake it. The time depends on the brand and the thickness of the clay. Bake twenty to thirty minutes for every ¼" (0.6cm) thickness. Underbaking can produce a sculpture that's hard on the surface but soft and weak within. It's better to bake a sculpture too long than not long enough.

Series Baking

Sometimes you'll bake a sculpture, or parts of it, more than once. In fact, every animal sculpture has at least two pre-baked parts—the eyeballs. The mouse has a pre-baked tail, the fox and fawn have pre-baked legs. Called series baking, this technique protects the shape of small, independently-modeled parts.

PROPPING
That wisp of white cloud beneath the bear is a baking prop. Made of cotton batting wrapped around a foil core, it will insure the bear won't slump in the oven. The cotton is soft enough to protect his texture, and the tightly packed foil strong enough to support his weight. Placing the thermometer next to the sculpture allows you to check the oven temperature where it matters most.

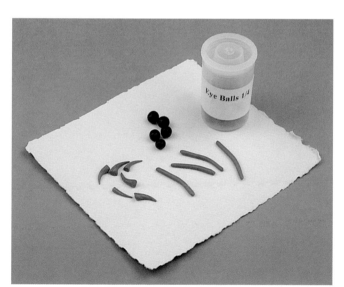

SERIES BAKING
Eyeballs and claws, fingers and toes—protect the shape of these small parts by baking them ahead of time. As long as you're making a pair of eyeballs, make and bake more than you need. Store them according to size or color.

Painting Techniques for Polymer Clay

Three painting techniques—dry brushing, washing and detailing—will heighten the reality you've created with shape and texture. Each technique has a special effect on the clay.

Dry Brushing

Dry brushing means just that, painting with dry bristles, barely dipped in paint. Wiping the brush on a paper towel dries the bristles even more. The brushstrokes should be light, grazing only the surface of a sculpture. This technique enhances textural details because the raised surface details are the only areas the paint touches. No paint flows into the crevices.

Dry brushing softens the texture of fur or feathers because the brush leaves a gentle dusting of pigment, not a solid coat.

Washing

A wash is a thin, transparent coat of paint that stains the dry brush coat and flows into the crevices, darkening both slightly. The underlying color of the clay and the effects of the dry brush coat will shine through, creating depth.

Detail Painting

Detail painting means using a small brush to paint small things. For example, if the dry brush and wash coats have covered the eyes, use the small brush to paint them black again, or to create a more defined iris.

The markings specific to an animal, such as the spots on the young fawn's back, are also details more easily done with a small brush.

Also use the small brush for final dry brushing if an animal is small, or if the area is small; for special washes in small areas, such as the ears, nose and mouth; and to scrub areas clean of paint to reveal the color of the clay, such as the rabbit's ears.

Varnishing the eyes, mouth and sometimes the nose is the final detail painting.

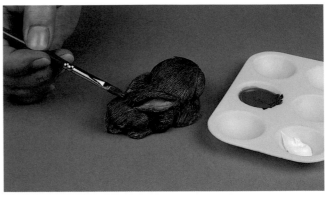

WASHING
Mix a small amount of paint with water to create a transparent stain. It should be the consistency of thin cream. Stain the entire animal. The wash coat will flow into the crevices, tinting both the base color (the color of the clay) and the dry brush coat. Two or three wash coats will deepen the color.

THE DETAIL COAT
Dry brushing more White paint brightened the fur around the rabbit's eyes and on his cheeks, whisker patches and paws. Black paint touched up his eyes and gloss varnish made them shine. All of these tasks are details usually done with a small brush.

DRY BRUSHING
Here is the rabbit with his first coat of paint — the dry brush coat. I used a dry, round bristle brush, dipping just the tip into White acrylic paint. Wiping the bristles back and forth on a folded paper towel removed most of the paint. Lightly brushing the surface of the sculpture leaves a dusting of pigment. No paint flows into the crevices. Every strand of fur is visible.

CHAPTER FOUR

Creating Animals Step by Step

The Deer Mouse

More than a dozen species of mice live in North America. Some, like the house mouse, are immigrants from Europe, but this fellow is a native. His slightly furry tail is a trait found only in North American mice. Prominent ears and large shining eyes give his sharp face a sweet expression. He sports a rich, reddish brown coat with a white underbelly. His hands and feet are white, too.

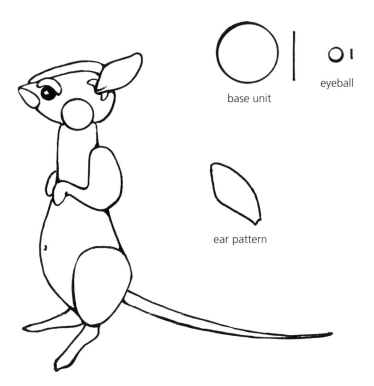

base unit

eyeball

ear pattern

This pattern guide shows the size, shape and placement of the component parts of the deer mouse. The line next to the base unit and the eyeball diagram illustrates the length of the slice if you choose the rod method for measuring the clay. The block method is illustrated below.

1 MEASURING THE CLAY

This is the block method for measuring the clay. Like the rod method, it will produce balls of clay a little larger than ⅜" (1.6cm) in diameter, the size of the base unit. Whichever method you choose, be sure your blade is straight and sharp.

You'll need two ounces (56.7g) of clay to complete this project. One ounce (28.4g)—or half a package—of Black clay is enough to make a stable base and the eyeballs. One ounce (28.4g) of Raw Sienna clay divided into eight equal sections is enough to make the mouse. When the instructions call for smaller amounts, divide the balls of clay as you need them, not all at once.

TIP

Follow the step-by-step instructions. Don't assemble the parts all at once. Assemble them one at time or in matching pairs. Blend the seams of each appliqué one at a time as you apply them.

TIP

If you use the block method to measure the clay and the clay is too soft, measure and divide the clay, then condition and leach each portion separately.

2 SHAPING THE HEAD AND SNOUT

The mouse's head begins as a tapered egg. Combine a ball and ¼ a ball of clay together into a smooth, round ball, then taper it in the hollow of your hand.

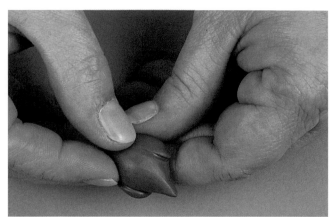

3 THE CHEEKS

Cut ¼ of a ball in half and roll each half into a ball. Flatten and attach them at the side of the head so that each cheek is positioned halfway between the tip of the nose and the back of the head. Work clay from the cheeks onto the head to blend the seams. The cheeks reduce in size, becoming well rounded.

4 A PROPER PROFILE

Shape ⅛ of a ball into a small cylinder about ⅝" (1.6cm) long. Flatten and apply it along the midline from the back of the head almost to the tip of the snout. Blend the seams by working clay from the cylinder onto the head.

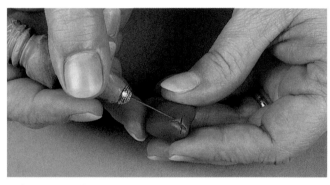

5 MARKING THE NOSE AND MOUTH

Use your finger to blunt the tip of the snout slightly. Use a fine needle to press an **X** on the tip of the snout.

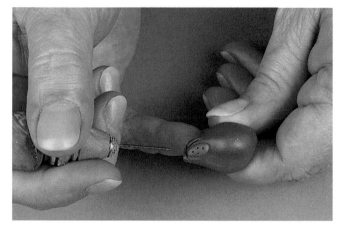

6 REFINING THE NOSE AND MOUTH

Make two small eggs of clay from balls about ⅛" (0.3cm) in diameter. Flatten and place one on each side of the **X** to form the upper lip. Don't blend the seams, just secure them in place. Poke three or four tiny follicles into the eggs.

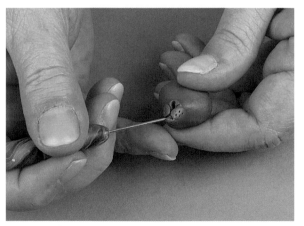

7

Open the mouth with the large tapestry needle and the nostrils with the smaller tapestry needle.

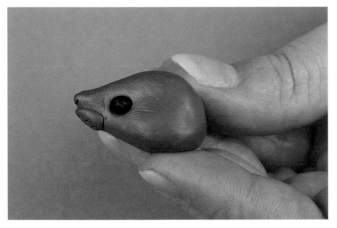

8 THE EYES AND LIDS

Use the rod method to measure a small amount of Black clay for eyeballs a little larger than ⅛" (0.3cm) in diameter. Bake the eyeballs for twenty minutes at 275° F. Place the eyes just behind the whisker patches, ⅓ of the way back from the tip of the nose and ⅔ up from the bottom of the cheeks.

9 Use two thin cylinders of clay about ¼" (0.6cm) long to shape the upper eyelids. Rotate the taper of a small knitting needle along the lid to blend the seam.

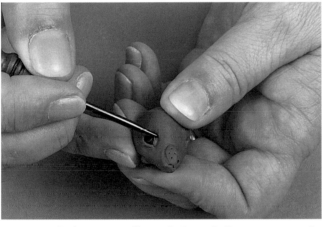

10 Let the knitting needle touch the eyeball as you suggest the lower lids by drawing a line below each eye.

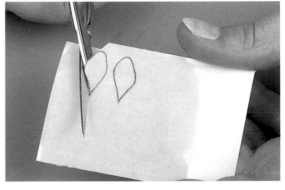

11 THE EARS

Trace the ear pattern from the pattern diagram on page 23 to a piece of card stock stiffened with Super Glue (see page 18). The glue-sized card will be transparent, making the pattern easy to trace.

12 Pinch each ear armature at the base to shape. Coat both sides of each armature with vinyl glue and let dry.

13 To cover an ear armature, pinch ⅛ of a ball of clay between your fingers to make a very thin pancake. Fold it over the armature to cover both sides. Press the clay-covered armature firmly between your fingers. Excess clay will tear off easily, leaving a nicely covered ear. Rub smooth with your finger.

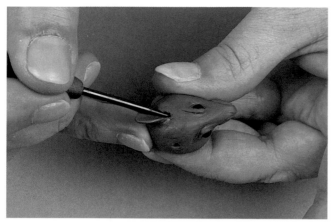

14 Use a medium knitting needle to pierce sockets behind each eye, halfway between the eye and the back of the head. Position each ear, using the needle to shape and secure them.

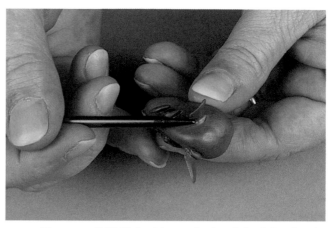

15 Place a small ¼" (0.6cm) long cylinder of clay behind each ear. Blend and seal the seam with a medium knitting needle.

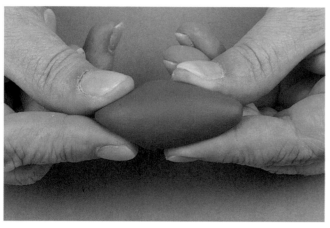

16 **SHAPING THE BODY**
Combine four balls of clay to form a smooth single ball, then an extended egg. Pinch the large end to form the pelvis.

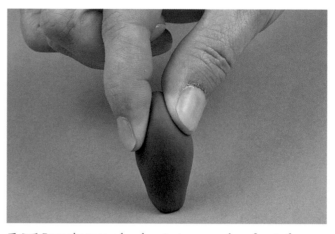

17 Press the tapered end against your work surface to form the neck.

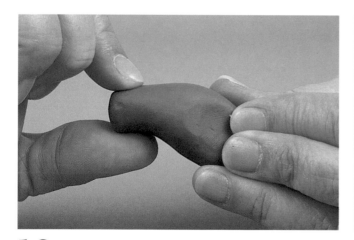

18 Arching the back creates a fat belly and rounded rump.

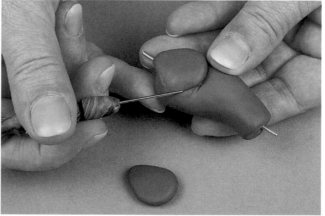

19 **THE HIND LEGS AND SPINE**
Make disks of two half balls of clay. Pinch each to form a teardrop shape. Attach securely to the pelvis. Use your thumb to blend the seam only where the thigh meets the rump. Add an extra fold of skin by creasing the clay with the small tapestry needle. Insert an armature rod into the body so that a bit more than ¼" (0.6cm) extends from the top and bottom. This "spine" will secure the mouse's head to his body and the mouse to the base.

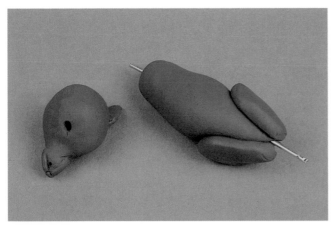

20 Pierce a hole at the bottom of the head, halfway between the ears and eyes and halfway between the cheeks.

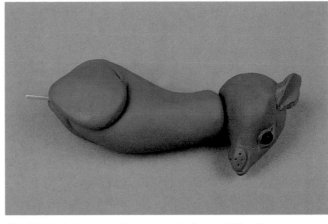

21 Push the head down onto the "spine." Blending the seams will model the neck and make the head just the right size.

22 MODELING THE NECK

Blend the back and side seams by working the clay from the back and sides of the head onto the body.

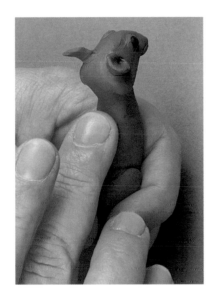

23 Work clay from the front of the mouse's body onto his lower jaw.

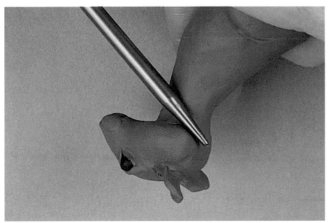

24 Use the shaft of the medium knitting needle to give the cheeks a more rounded outline

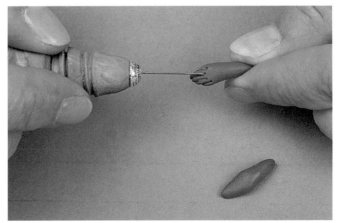

25 THE FEET

Cut ⅛ of a ball in half and roll each half to form a ½" (1.3cm) cylinder. Gently flatten and taper one end to form the toe. Mark five toes on each foot with a fine needle. Mark the two outside toes first, then the inside toes.

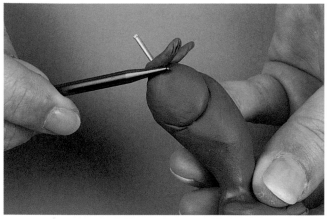

26 Position each foot and press into place. Blend the seam, first on the inside, then the outside and back of each ankle with the tip of a knitting needle.

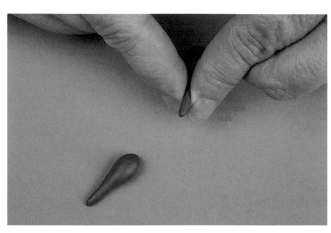

27 THE ARMS AND HANDS
Shape two quarter balls of clay so they resemble small clubs about 1" (2.5cm) long. Roll the forearm between two fingers to create the wrist and the hand.

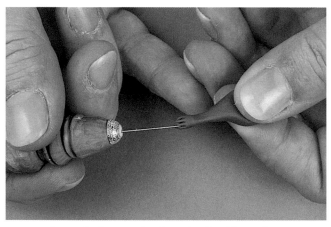

28 Flatten the large end to form the shoulder and upper arm. Flatten the hand slightly. Use a fine needle to mark the fingers on each hand by pressing the needle almost all the way through. Mark the middle first, then divide each to create four definite fingers. The mouse's thumb, which is almost an opposed thumb, is not visible.

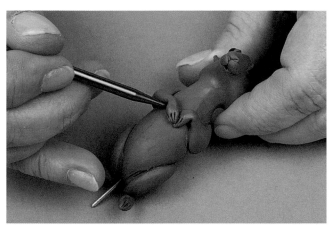

29 Attach the arms by pressing the upper arm firmly in place. Pose the forearms and hands, using a knitting needle to obtain a crook in the wrist.

30 Blend the seams of the arms where the shoulder joins the body by working clay from the shoulder and upper arms onto the mouse's back.

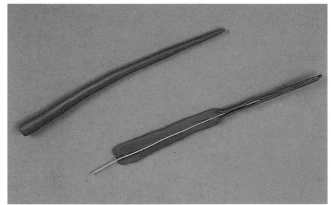

31 THE MOUSE'S TAIL
Combine the leftover clay to make the tail. Roll a narrowly extended cone about 3" (7.6cm) long and press flat. Coat 3" (7.6cm) of beading wire with vinyl glue and let dry. Center the wire armature on the flattened tail. Fold the tail over the wire.

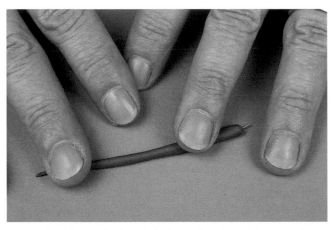

32 Roll the tail back and forth gently to blend the seam. You may need to do a little shaping at the tip.

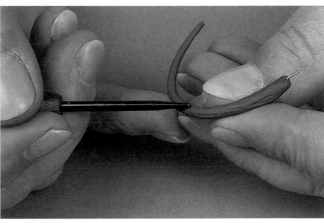

33 Curl the tail. Use the small knitting needle to draw short, furry lines from the base to the tip. Bake on an index card in a glass pan for twenty minutes at 275° F and let cool.

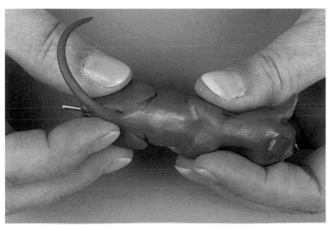

34 Make a starter hole at the base of the mouse's rump and insert the tail. Work clay from the mouse's rump onto his tail to hide the joint. Let your mouse rest while you make the base.

35 **A LITTLE PATCH OF EARTH**
Roll one ounce (28.4g) of Black clay into a ball and flatten until the ball is a little more than ¼" (0.6cm) thick. Roll a crumpled wad of aluminum foil over the base to give it a rough, earthy texture. Use a rod the same size as the "spine" to poke a hole in the base where your mouse will stand. Rotating the rod insures the hole remains large enough. Sign your name on the base, then bake it for twenty minutes at 275° F.

TEXTURE PATTERNS
The mouse's fur follows the contours of his body. It radiates away from his nose and eyes, grows toward the back of his head, then down the back of his body. The belly fur radiates toward his navel. Don't texture the whisker patches that form his upper lip, or his hands and feet.

TIP
Some sculptures are large or stable enough to stand on their own. The deer mouse needs a secure platform so he won't topple when people touch him— and people will want to touch him.

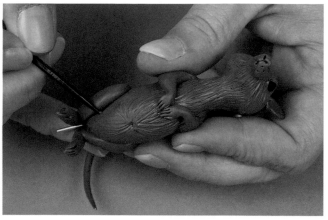

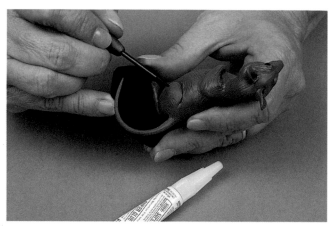

36 CREATING A FURRY TEXTURE

Use a small knitting needle to draw closely-spaced, furry lines. The faster you work, the lighter your strokes will be. Do the head, neck and upper chest first. Create the navel by dimpling the clay. Take care around the arms and hands when you texture the belly. Texture the back, then place the mouse on the base before you finish the fur on his thighs and arms.

37 PUTTING THE MOUSE ON SOLID GROUND

Insert the spine into the hole in the base and gently press down. A little Super Glue in the hole helps secure the mouse. Position the tail so that the tip rests on the base, using glue to hold it in place, if necessary. Hold your sculpture by the base as you finish texturing. Then, check the details, redrawing any of the furry lines that got smudged. Letting him rest an hour before baking will improve the bond between baked and unbaked clay. Bake him for sixty minutes in a glass pan at 275° F and let cool.

Painting the Mouse

Twenty-two carefully shaped pieces assembled just so and you've created a brown mouse with black eyes on a black base. But he's not quite finished yet. Three painting techniques—dry brushing, washing and detail painting—will bring him to life.

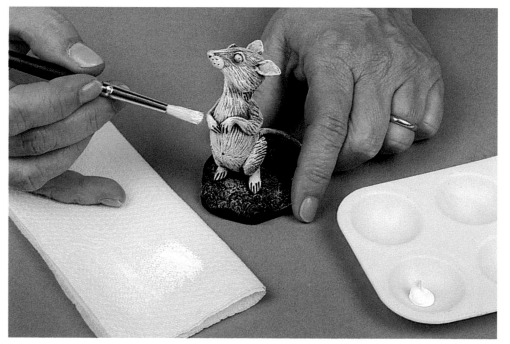

38 DRY BRUSHING

Use a no. 3 round bristle brush and Titanium White paint to dry brush the mouse. Wipe the brush on a paper towel to remove most of the paint. It's better to have too little paint than too much as you lightly brush across the grain of the fur. Paint the entire mouse until every strand of fur is visible. Pay special attention to the lower jaw, belly, inner thighs, the hands and feet, inner ears, mouth and nose. These areas need an extra dry brush coat. Let dry thoroughly, about thirty minutes.

The dry brushing completed.

39 THE WASH COAT

Blend equal amounts of Raw Sienna and Raw Umber, and add a little water to make a staining wash the consistency of thin cream. Stain the entire mouse lightly and let dry. Stain his back, hind legs, arms and the back and top of his head two more times, letting the paint dry in between coats.

40 PAINTING THE DETAILS

Use the no. 1 bristle brush and Titanium White paint to highlight the dry brush coat on the lower jaw, belly, thighs, hands and feet, mouth and nose, and the underside of his tail. Use the no. 00 synthetic brush to paint his eyes Black. Mix a pink wash of Raw Sienna, Cadmium Red Medium and Titanium White. Test your wash on a sheet of paper for transparency and hue before tinting his nose and mouth. Tinting the inside of his ears with the same pink wash will create the illusion of ears so thin the light shines through them. When the detail paint is dry, varnish his bottom lip and eyes with a glossy acrylic varnish.

The Young Cottontail

Born naked, with his eyes tightly closed, the cottontail kit is totally dependent on his mother. In two weeks time, he can leave the nest. Camouflaged by a soft gray-brown coat, the young cottontail can explore the surrounding thicket, but spends most of his time sleeping. Meanwhile, other rabbits linger nearby, their high-set eyes aware of every shifting shadow, their large ears alert to every sound... .

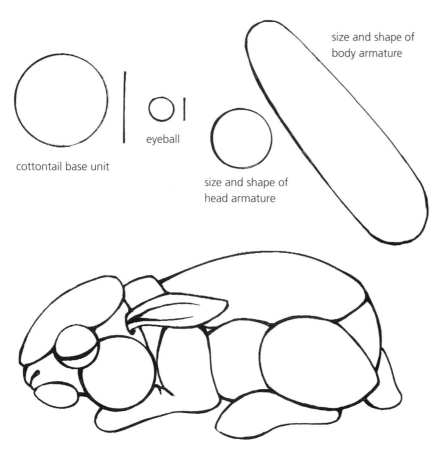

cottontail base unit

eyeball

size and shape of
head armature

size and shape of
body armature

Like the deer mouse, the young cottontail—and its two foil armature—is made of simple shapes. Like the mouse, this sculpture's overall contours depend on how the appliqués are put together and blended.

WHAT YOU'LL NEED FOR THIS PROJECT

Polymer Clay
- Ecru
- Raw Sienna
- prebaked eyeballs made from Black clay, ¼" (0.6cm) in diameter

Armature
- 4" × 8" (10.2cm × 20.3cm) strip of aluminum foil
- 2' (61cm) length of aluminum foil

Tools
- blade for cutting the clay
- ruler
- fine needle tool
- small and large tapestry needle tools
- small, medium and large knitting needles
- pasta machine or roller
- small hammer

Acrylic Paints
- Black
- Raw Umber
- Titanium White

Brushes
- no. 00 synthetic
- no. 1 and no. 3 round bristle brushes
- no. 6 synthetic round or filbert

Other Supplies
- paint mixing tray or four small jar lids
- paper towel for wiping dry brush
- vinyl glue (Sobo, Gem Tac or Aleene's Tacky)
- gloss varnish

1 MEASURING AND MIXING THE CLAY

To make a cottontail the same size and color as the one on page 32, you'll need three ounces (85.1g) of Ecru clay and 1½ ounces (42.5g) of Raw Sienna clay (twice as much Ecru as Raw Sienna). Divide each color into twelve sections, then combine one section of Raw Sienna with one section of Ecru and roll into a 1" (2.5cm) diameter ball. This is the base unit for the cottontail. Continue to combine one section of each of the two colors and roll into balls until you have ten balls. Save the leftover clay for another project.

TIP

There's no need to condition your clay if you're mixing colors. By the time you thoroughly blend different colors with no marbling, the clay is conditioned. Don't forget to leach the clay after you've blended your custom color. It will be firmer and much easier to control.

2 SHAPING A ROUND FOIL CORE

To shape a round foil core, fold a 4" × 8" (10.2cm × 20.3cm) sheet of foil into a 4" (10.2cm) square. Gather two sides together in the center to make a bow tie (above), then gather the other sides together to make a butterfly (top right). Crumple the "wings" toward the center and press firmly. Roll the foil ball firmly against a tabletop, or use a small hammer (right) to make it very round and smooth. The ball should be the same size as the armature diagram on page 33.

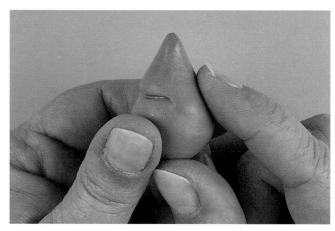

3 COVERING A ROUND CORE

Wrap a disk made of ¾ of a ball of the Raw Sienna/Ecru mixture around the foil core. Blend the seams and roll the ball gently in your hands until it is the same size as the base unit.

4 SHAPING THE BASIC HEAD

Apply a cone made from ¼ of a ball of clay to the covered core. Blend the seams by working clay from the cone onto the ball. You'll use this basic head shape quite often. Except for its construction, it's the same shape you modeled for the deer mouse's head

5 Snub the tip of the cone with your finger to begin shaping the nose.

TIP

For very small fractions of clay, such as ¹⁄₃₂ of a ball, you'll find it easier to divide the clay accurately if you begin with ¼ of a ball. Slice a ball into four parts, then roll one of these quarters into a ball before cutting this section into fourths again (¼ of a quarter ball is ¹⁄₁₆ of a full ball, and so on).

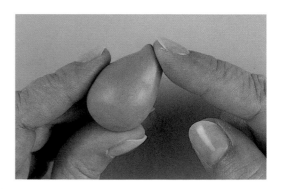

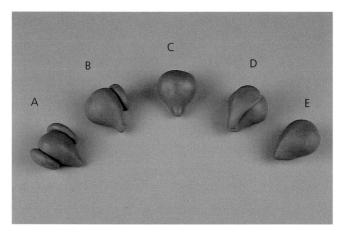

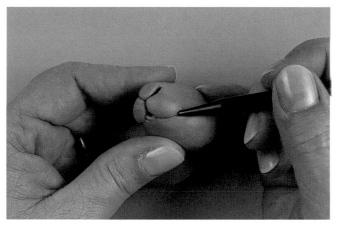

6 BUILDING THE CHEEKS AND PROFILE

The above picture shows all the steps necessary to build the cheeks and profile. For the cheeks, apply ¼ of a ball formed into a disk to each side of the head (A). Blend the seams between the cheeks and head piece (B and C). To build the profile, roll a 1¼" (3.2cm) long elongated egg from ¼ of a ball of clay and flatten. Attach along the midline from the tip of the nose to the back of the head (D). Blend the seams (E).

7 THE NOSE AND MOUTH

Press a **Y** on the tip of the nose with a fine needle. Open the nostrils with the small tapestry needle and the mouth with a small knitting needle. Use ½ of a ball for each whisker patch. Roll these balls into eggs, flatten slightly and apply one on each side of the **Y**. Outline the edge of each patch with a knitting needle to seal the seams.

8 THE EYES AND LIDS

Use the rod method (page 14) to measure a small amount of Black clay; use this to make two ¼" (0.6cm) diameter eyeballs. Bake the eyeballs for twenty minutes at 275° F. Place the eyeballs behind the whisker patches and push a little more than halfway into the clay.

Use ½ of a ball for each pair of eyelids. Roll into a ball, then pinch to form thin, round pancakes. Cut each into two semicircles, one larger than the other. Apply the lower lids first, using the smaller semicircles. Apply the larger semicircle as the upper eyelids. Blend the seams with the taper of a large knitting needle.

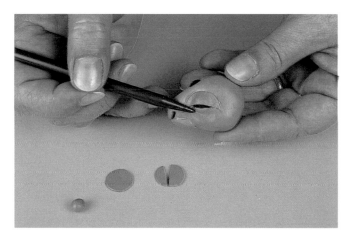

9 SHAPING THE FOIL CORE FOR THE BODY

Use a sheet of foil 2' long × 8" wide (61cm × 20.3cm) to form a core to fill the body. Fold in half lengthwise, making it 4" (10.2cm) wide. Gather and begin crumpling into shape (above left). Crimp the large end where the foil was folded (above right), then finish crumpling. Firmly press the core into shape until it matches the body armature diagram on page 33.

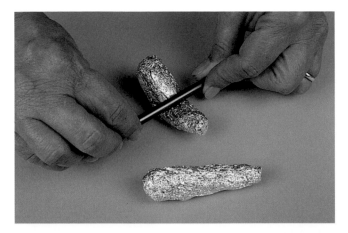

TIP

This is a compact sculpture. It doesn't need a base to protect it, or an armature to support it. The foil armature in the body and head aren't necessary, but they are practical. They save clay and baking time—almost two ounces (56.7g) of clay and two hours of baking time.

10 Press the center of the core against the edge of a table or the shaft of a large knitting needle to bend slightly.

11 **COVERING THE BODY ARMATURE**
Use ¾ of a ball for the first layer of clay. Press small pieces of clay into the more pronounced crevices, then press additional pieces in place. Use your thumb to rub each piece smooth, plastering the surface with a uniform layer of clay.

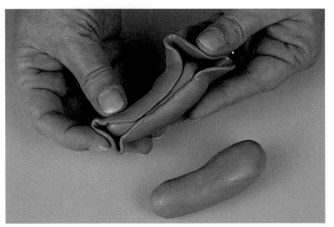

12 Combine 1¼ balls of clay. Form an egg, then press or roll it into an oval pancake 3½" wide × 4" long × ⅛" thick (8.9cm × 10.2cm × 0.3cm). Note that this wrapping layer is slightly longer and about three times the diameter of the core. Stretch the pancake as you wrap it around the core, pulling the seams together. Blend the seams and rub to create a smooth, basic body.

TIP

You can cover the body armature in a single step by combining the clay for the plaster layer and the wrapping layer together (steps 11 and 12 in this project). However, the foil core must be properly prepared or disaster will follow: Air pockets can form between the clay and core that will cause significant bubbles and ruptures during baking.

To use the single wrap method, the armature must be smooth and free of substantial crevices and treated with a vinyl glue. A smooth foil core ensures a smooth wrap. Coating the core with vinyl glue insures the clay sticks to the foil. Let the glue dry, then wrap with clay.

You may find this technique a little difficult because you have to shape a larger amount of clay into a smooth body, but it's a skill well worth mastering.

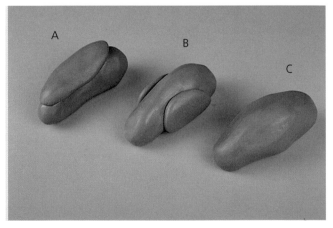

13 **BUILDING UP THE BODY**
Three appliqués shape the cottontail's body. The first, a flattened egg made from a ball of clay, builds up the back (A). Blend the seams from the first appliqué before you add the oval disks to the sides. These disks create a slightly bulging belly. Use a half ball for each disk of belly fat (B). Blend the seams (C).

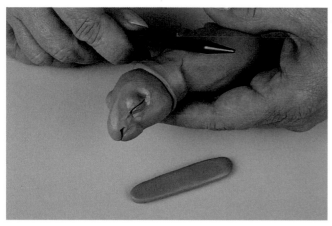

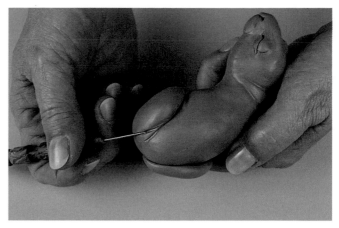

14 **ATTACHING THE HEAD AND MODELING THE NECK**
When you attach the head to the tapered end of the body, work clay from the body onto the head, then add a collar like the one shown here. It's made from ¼ of a ball of clay rolled into a 2" (5.1cm) long cylinder. Flatten and wrap the collar around the neck. Use the shaft of a large knitting needle as a roller to blend the seam, but don't overblend.

15 **THE HIND LEGS**
Make two teardrop-shaped disks, each from a ½ ball of clay. Attach so that the tapered end faces the cottontail's rump. Blend the seam only where the thigh meets the rump. Add extra folds of skin by creasing the clay with a tapestry needle.

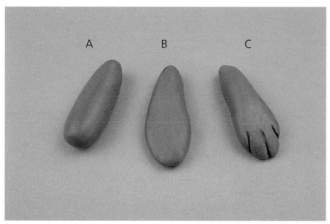

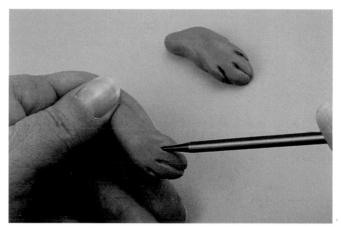

16 **THE HIND FEET**
Use ⅜ of a ball for each hind foot. Cut a full ball into fourths and set aside ¼ of the ball for the ears. Roll the three remaining quarters together and cut in half. Shape each half into an extended egg, 1½" (3.8cm) long (A). Flatten the large end, then pinch slightly to form the toe of the foot. Curve each, making a right and left foot (B). Use a fine needle to mark four toes on each foot (C).

17 Use a small knitting needle to enhance the cleft between each toe. Pinch the toes gently to refine the overall shape of the foot.

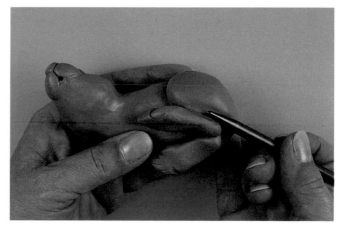

18 Position the hind feet at the base of the thigh. Roll the shaft of a knitting needle over the seam to secure them.

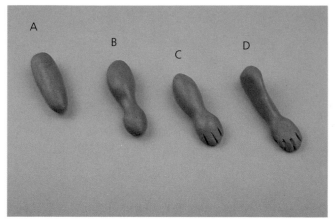

19 THE FRONT LIMBS AND PAWS

Each forelimb begins with half of a ball rolled into an extended egg, 1½" (3.8cm) long (A). Suggest a forearm, wrist and paw by gently rolling the egg between your fingers near the small end to form a club (B). Flatten the handle to shape a paw. Use the fine needle to mark four toes (C) and the large tapestry needle to enhance the cleft between each toe (D).

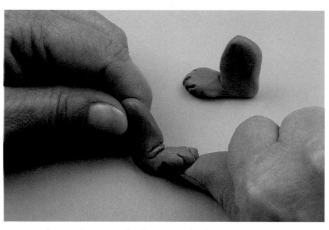

20

Flatten the upper limb perpendicular to the paw. Bend the limb in the middle, creating an elbow. Use the shaft of a small knitting needle to define folds in the skin.

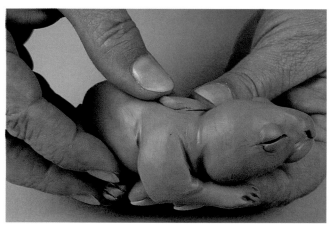

21

Attach the limbs to the body just behind the head. Blend the seams by working the clay up onto the back, creating shoulders in the process. Use the tapestry needle to create folds in the skin at the armpit. Position the paws beneath the head.

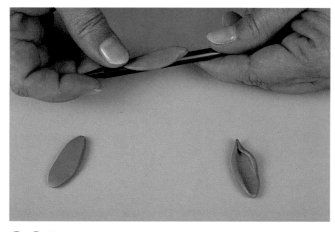

22 THE EARS

Use ⅛ of a ball of clay for each ear. Form an extended egg 1⅛" long (2.9cm). Flatten, then shape over a large knitting needle. Pinch the small end of each ear to form the base.

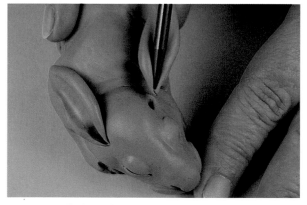

23

Use the large knitting needle to create an ear socket behind each eye, halfway between the eye and the back of the head. Insert the ears into the sockets using a large knitting needle to hold, secure and shape.

24 MAKING THE TAIL

Begin the tail by tapering both ends of an egg made from ⅛ of a ball of clay. Bend the tail by curling it over your fingertip.

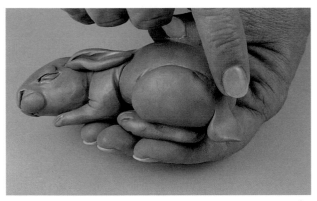

25 Attach the tail at the base of the rump. Blend only the top seam, but make sure it is secure.

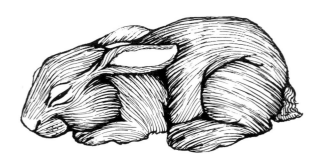

TEXTURE PATTERNS

The cottontail's fur follows the same growth patterns as the mouse's: parallel to the length of the body, curving toward the belly on the sides. The fur on the limbs runs parallel to the bones. On the ears, it grows from the base toward the tip. This pattern of growth is true for most mammals.

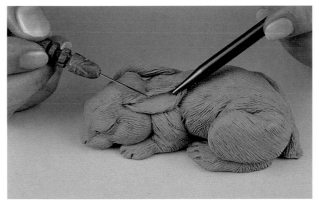

26 CREATING THE TEXTURE
Following the texture pattern, use the small tapestry needle to draw long, smooth strokes to suggest sleek, soft fur. Do not texture the tip of the nose, nor the insides of the ears. Use a large knitting needle to hold the ears in place when you texture them. Draw short, wavy strokes on the tail. When finished, bake in a glass baking pan for 1½ hours at 275° F.

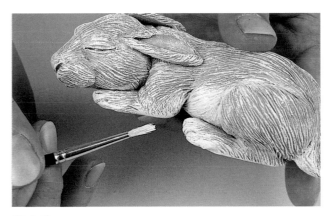

27 DRY BRUSHING THE COTTONTAIL
Use a no. 3 round bristle brush and Titanium White paint to dry brush the cottontail. The eyelids, whisker patches, and the outer rim of each ear require an extra dry brush coat. The belly fur on the cottontail's sides, the inner thighs, the sides of the tail and all four feet also need an extra coat. Rub your finger on the tip of the nose to remove some of the dry brush.

28 APPLYING THE WASH
Mix one part Black and two parts Raw Umber with a little water and stain the entire sculpture. Let dry and apply a second wash. Before the second wash dries, use a clean, damp (not wet) brush to lift stain from the ears, the sides of the belly, the feet, the eyes and the tail.

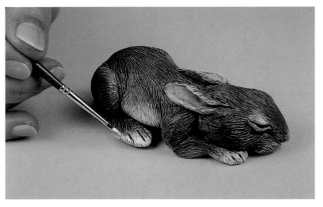

29 THE DETAIL COAT
Using a no. 00 synthetic brush, touch up the sides of the tail and the visible belly fur. Use the small bristle brush to dry brush the tips of the paws, the whisker patches and the edges of the ears with Titanium White. Touch up the eyeballs with Black paint and make them shine with gloss varnish.

The Harp Seal

Within three weeks of birth, a short, silvery coat flecked with small, dark spots will replace the thick white fur of this harp seal's infancy. In time, he will develop a black, harp-shaped band across his back, the hallmark that gives the species its name. For the moment, this week-old pup is a "white back," with fur so remarkable it absorbs ultraviolet light.

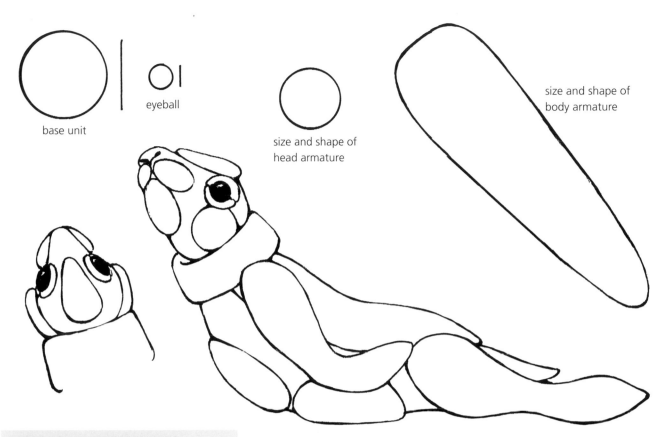

base unit

eyeball

size and shape of
head armature

size and shape of
body armature

WHAT YOU'LL NEED FOR THIS PROJECT

Polymer Clay
- Ecru
- White
- prebaked eyeballs made from Black clay ¼" (0.6cm) in diameter

Armature
- 3' (91.4cm) length of aluminum foil
- 4" x 8" (10.2cm x 20.3cm) sheet of aluminum foil
- 1–2" (2.5–5.1cm) brass rod

Tools
- blade for cutting the clay
- ruler
- fine needle tool
- small and large tapestry needles
- small, medium and large knitting needles
- small hammer

Acrylic Paints
- Black
- Raw Umber
- Titanium White

Brushes
- no. 00 synthetic
- no. 1 and no. 3 round bristle brushes
- no. 6 synthetic round or filbert

Other Supplies
- paint mixing tray or small jar lids
- paper towel for wiping dry brush
- gloss varnish

The harp seal sculpture uses many of the same shapes you used to model the young cottontail. The cheeks and profile are smaller, but applied in the same way onto the same basic head. Though the seal and cottontail are very different animal sculptures, you'll be surprised by their similarities.

1 MEASURING AND MIXING THE CLAY

The base color for the harp seal is a custom blend of two ounces (56.7g) Titanium White and two ounces (56.7g) Ecru. Divide each block into twelve sections and blend each section of white with a section of Ecru. Roll the blended clay into twelve balls, ⅞" (2.2cm) in diameter, the base unit for the harp seal. This project uses a little less than ten balls of clay

TIP
It's hard to keep light-colored clays clean. To protect them from dark smudges and tiny fibers:
- Clean your work space, hands and tools before you begin.
- Clean your hands often, especially after working with foil.
- Put the dog or cat out.
- Don't wear a sweater.
- Cover your seal with a lint-free cloth or tissue paper when you're not working on it.

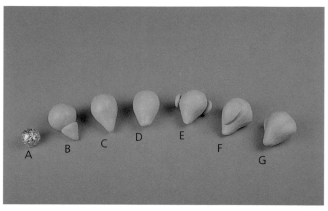

2 BUILDING A BASIC HEAD OVER A FOIL CORE

Use a 4" × 8" (10.2cm × 20.3cm) sheet of foil to form a round foil core identical to the cottontail's (A). Cover with a disk made of ¾ of a ball. Attach a cone made of ¼ of a ball (B) and blend the seams (C). Snub the tip with your finger to begin shaping the nose (D). Use ¹⁄₁₆ of a ball for each cheek (E). Blend. To build the profile, form a teardrop from ⅛ of a ball and flatten. Center on top of head (F) and blend (G).

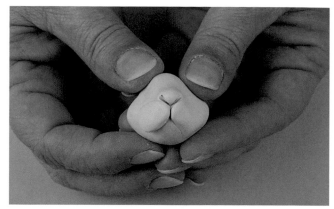

3 THE NOSE, MOUTH AND WHISKER PATCHES

Press a **Y** on the tip of the nose with a fine needle. Open the nostrils with a tapestry needle. Define the mouth by pressing a wide, upside down **V** at the base of the **Y** with a small tapestry needle. The unblended patch on the left shows you the size and position of this small appliqué. The blended patch on the right shows you how a properly blended patch should look. Use flattened eggs made of ¹⁄₁₆ of a ball for each.

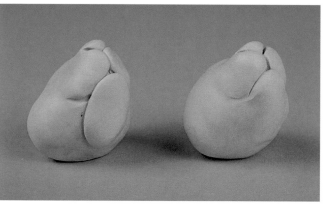

4 THE LOWER JAW

To create the chin, use a flattened egg made from ⅛ of a ball of clay. Apply so that it just touches the bottom lip (left). Blend only the bottom seam (right).

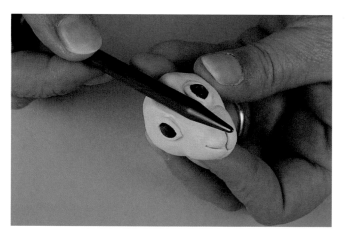

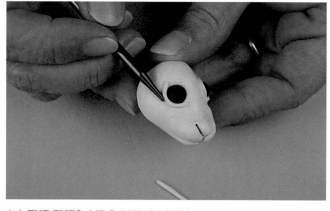

5 THE EYES, LIDS AND BROWS

Use the rod method to measure a small amount of Black clay for ¼" (0.6cm) diameter eyeballs. Bake for twenty minutes at 275° F. Place the eyeballs behind the whisker patches, midway between the tip of the nose and the back of the head. The foil core should keep you from pushing them in too deeply. Use four thin rods of clay about ½" (1.2cm) long to shape the upper and lower eyelids—¹⁄₃₂ of a ball is more than enough clay for these rods. Apply the lower lids first, then attach the upper eyelids. Blend the seams with the tapered end of a medium knitting needle.

6 To create brow ridges, gently press the shaft of a large knitting needle against the forehead.

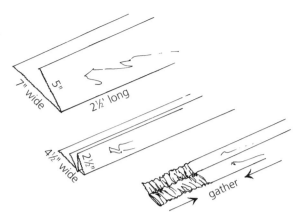

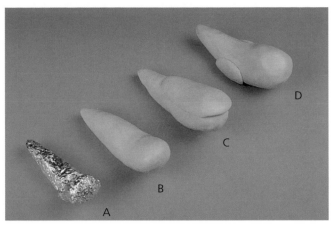

7 SHAPING THE BODY ARMATURE

To shape the body armature, use a 2½' long × 1' wide (76cm × 30cm) sheet of foil. Fold a 5" (12.7cm) section in on the 1' (30cm) width, making the sheet 7" wide × 2 ½' long (17.8cm × 76cm). Fold another 2½" (6.4cm) in, widthwise, making the sheet 4½" (11.4cm) wide. Gather the foil lengthwise, then crumple and press the folded foil into shape, using the same method you used for the cottontail's armature (page 35). It should match the body armature diagram on page 11.

8 SHAPING THE BODY

Bend the foil core 1" (2.5cm) from the large end by pressing it against the edge of a table (A). Use one ball of clay to plaster the foil with small pieces. Use 1½ balls to make an oval pancake ⅛" (0.3cm) thick. Wrap the pancake around the body and blend the seams (B). This is the basic body. Build up the back and shoulders with an egg-shaped pancake made of 1½ balls of clay, overlapping the large end of the body (C). Blend the seams. Add oval disks to round out the sides of the belly, using ⅛ of a ball for each (D).

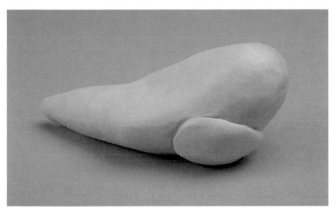

9

After blending the sides of the belly, apply an oval disk made from half of a ball to the base of the chest. This will give the sculpture more shape and stability. Blend the seams.

10 ATTACHING THE HEAD AND MODELING THE NECK

Pierce the back of the head and the neck with a tapestry needle, making sure to pierce each foil core. Bend a 1" (2.5cm) brass rod in the center slightly. Insert it into the neck until only half of the rod is exposed. Holding the head gently, push it onto the rod until it touches the neck. Work clay from the body onto the head to secure.

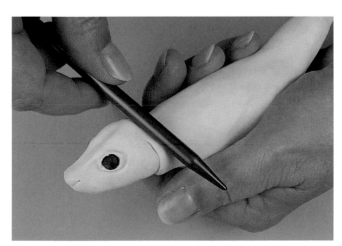

11

Use ¾ of a ball to form a flat collar 4" long × ⅝" wide (10.2cm × 1.6cm). Wrap around the neck. Blend the seams by working clay from the collar onto the body, then onto the head. Don't blend away the shape of the jaws.

12 SHAPING THE TAIL

With your thumb and fingers, pull the tail to a dull point. Press the shaft of a small knitting needle against the sides, making the tail about ½" (1.3cm) long.

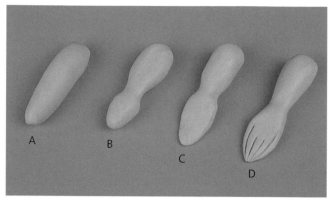

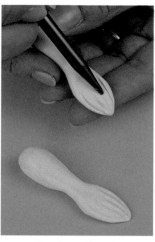

13 THE HIND FLIPPERS

Use ¾ of a ball of clay for each hind flipper. Shape an extended egg 1¾" long (4.5cm) (A). Roll between your fingers to shape a club (B). Gently pinch the "handle" to flatten, then elongate and caress it to a point with your fingers (C). Use a fine needle to mark the longer outer toes, creating a curved **V**. Mark the shorter inner toes next (D).

14 Gentle strokes along these lines with a medium knitting needle will round the toes.

15 Use the large tapestry needle to enhance the cleft between each toe about ¼" (0.6cm) from the tips.

16 Flatten the thigh and attach it so the flipper lays against the tail. Work clay from the thigh onto the hips and back. Take care not to obscure the base of the tail as you blend the seams.

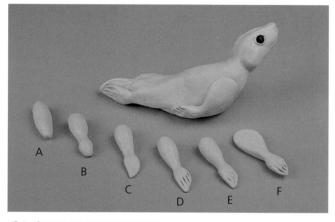

17 THE FRONT FLIPPERS

The front flippers are made using the same technique as the back flippers, except they are shaped more like paws. Use half of a ball for each. Shape an extended egg (A) into a club (B). Gently pinch and shape the "handle" to form an angled chisel (C). Beginning with the little "finger", mark five fingers with the fine needle (D). Stroke each line with the large knitting needle to round out the fingers (E). Define each cleft with the large tapestry needle about ⅛" (0.3cm) to ¼" (0.6cm) from the tips.

18 Flatten the upper limb and attach to the side, near the neck. Blend the seams by working the clay up onto the shoulder blades. Lay the flippers against the body and secure.

TEXTURE PATTERNS

The seal's thick fur follows the same pattern of growth as the mouse and cottontail. Notice the angled lines on the "fingers" and "toes" of the flippers. The fur grows toward the tips of the flippers, but marking it at an angle will accent your careful modeling.

19 TEXTURING THE BODY AND HEAD
Use the large tapestry needle to mark five rows of follicles on each whisker patch. Use the large knitting needle to dimple the eyebrow follicles and the ears.

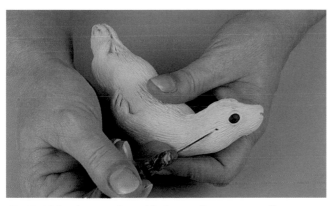

20 Make short strokes with the small tapestry needle to create the illusion of thick fur. Work gently around the brows and ears—don't obscure them, but don't avoid them, either. Always use a follicle as the starting point for each whisker. Don't texture the tip of the nose, the lower lip or eyelids.

21 BAKING AND DRY BRUSHING THE HARP SEAL
Bake the seal in a glass baking pan for one hour at 275° F. Propping the head with wadded aluminum foil wrapped in cotton batting will prevent stress cracks in the neck. Cool, then apply a white dry brush coat to the entire animal. Let dry.

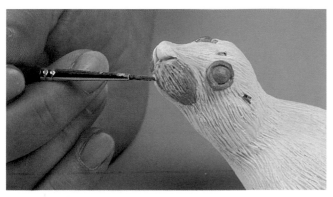

22 THE WASH AND COLOR COATS
Apply a white wash on the seal's back and head to brighten the fur. Let dry. Blend Titanium White, Black and Raw Umber to make a soft, warm gray. Use the small brush to paint the eyelids, brow follicles, ears and whisker patches.

23 THE DETAIL COAT
Dry brush the whisker patches with white to soften them. Touch up the fur around the eyelids, if necessary. Touch up the eyes with black paint. Paint the nose and lips black; it may take two or three coats to achieve opaque coverage. Let each coat dry thoroughly to prevent streaking. Varnish the eyes, eyelids, nose and lips with gloss varnish.

PROJECT FOUR

The Black Bear

The smallest of the North American bears, the black bear is also the most successful. These resourceful animals have developed a capacity to live close to us. In the pine forests of the West and the hardwood forests of the East, they tolerate our invasion of their territory with wit and imagination. In the Great Smoky Mountains—where "bear proof" dumpsters are the law and feeding bears is illegal—black bears have learned to pick the locks on dumpsters, rattle soda machines until the cans roll free and arrive at picnics just in time for dessert.

From armatures to appliqués, this sculpture uses old and new techniques. You'll use an old technique to make the head armature and a new technique, called wrapping, to shape the body armature. To build up the profile, you'll use a strip that also shapes the back of the skull. To build up the muzzle, you'll use a single strip rather than a pair of appliqués. What looks like a collar for securing the bear's head to the body is actually a fat disk that shapes the neck. If the bear were lying down, his belly would bulge at the sides like the rabbit's or seal's. This bear is standing, so you'll use a single appliqué to create a fat belly that bulges slightly at the sides and hangs down.

WHAT YOU'LL NEED FOR THIS PROJECT

Polymer Clay
- Burnt Umber
- prebaked eyeballs made from Black clay, or ball bearings, ⅛" (0.3cm) in diameter

Armature
- 2½" (6.4cm) length of aluminum foil
- 6" × 12" (15.2cm × 30.5cm) sheet of aluminum foil
- four 12" × 12" (30.5cm × 30.5cm) sheets of aluminum foil
- four 2¼" (5.7cm) metal rods
- card stock sized with Super Glue

Tools
- blade for cutting the clay
- ruler
- fine needle tool
- small and large tapestry needle tools
- small, medium and large knitting needles
- small hammer

Acrylic Paints
- Black
- Raw Sienna
- Titanium White

Brushes
- no. 00 synthetic
- no. 1 and no. 3 round bristle brushes
- no. 6 synthetic round or filbert

Other Supplies
- paint mixing tray or small jar lids
- paper towel for wiping dry brush
- cyanoacrylate glue (Super Glue)
- vinyl glue (Sobo, Gem Tac or Aleene's Tacky)
- gloss varnish

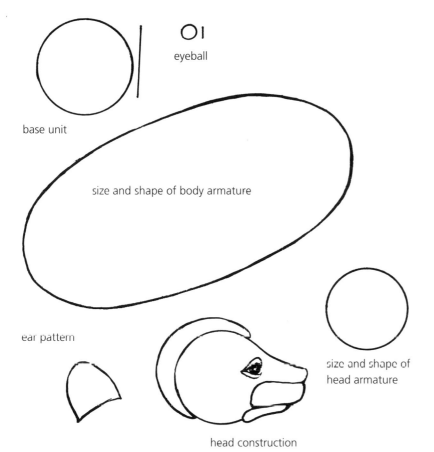

base unit

eyeball

size and shape of body armature

ear pattern

size and shape of head armature

head construction

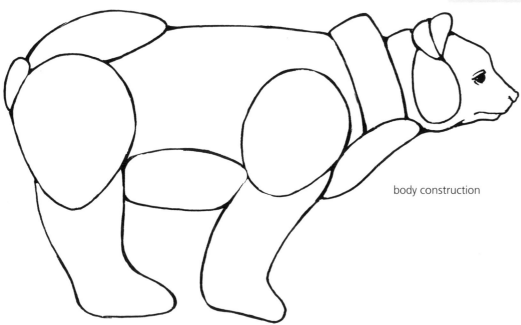

body construction

1 MEASURING THE CLAY

The base color for the black bear is Burnt Umber. You'll need four two-ounce (56.7g) packages of clay. Divide each package into sixteen sections, then combine three sections together. Each package will yield 5⅓ 1" (2.5cm) diameter balls, the base unit for the bear. This project uses a bit more than twenty balls of clay.

3 SHAPING THE MUZZLE AND EYE SOCKETS

Pinch the muzzle gently. As you pinch, pressure from your thumb and finger should create hollows on each side of the muzzle. These hollows are the eye sockets.

5 THE LOWER JAW

Form an egg from ¹⁄₁₆ of a ball. Flatten the egg slightly and apply it to the bottom of the muzzle. Create the chin by pressing the shaft of a large knitting needle across the lower jaw where the muzzle meets the face.

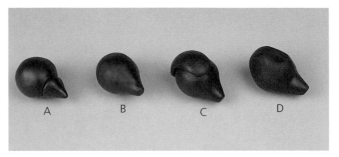

2 BUILDING THE BASIC HEAD OVER A FOIL CORE

Use a 6" × 12" (15.2cm × 30.4cm) sheet of foil to form a round foil core ⅞" (2.2cm) in diameter. Cover with a thin disk made of half a ball. Attach a cone made of ⅛ of a ball (A) and blend the seams. Snub the tip of the nose by pressing it against a flat surface (B). Use a quarter ball to make a strip 1½" × ¾" (3.8cm × 1.9cm) and apply to the top of the head so that it wraps around to the back of the head (C). Blend the seams, then flatten the top of the head slightly (D).

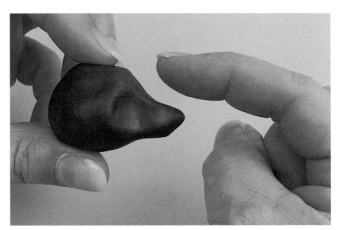

4 Stroke toward the tip of the nose to flatten the top of the muzzle.

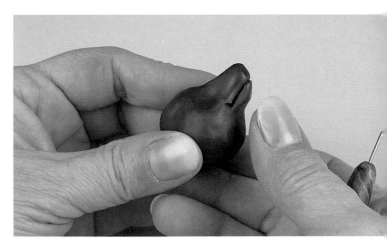

6 Pinch the lower jaw gently to refine its shape. Mark the corners of the mouth with a small tapestry needle, then blend the seam.

7 THE UPPER JAW

Shape a ¾" (1.9cm) long rod from ⅟₁₆ of a ball. Flatten and wrap around the muzzle so it barely overlaps the lower jaw. Blend the top seams carefully, reshaping the nose and eye sockets, if necessary. Blend the bottom seams up to the corners of the mouth.

8

Use a medium knitting needle to define the sides of the muzzle where it meets the face.

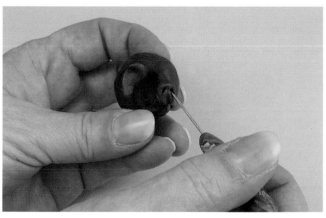

9 MARKING THE NOSE

With the large tapestry needle, press a gentle groove in the middle of the lip, but don't split it. Press a diagonal groove on the sides of the nose. Each nostril has a unique U-shaped cleft. Mark half of each cleft on the front of the nose with the small tapestry needle. Widen this part of the cleft by moving the needle around.

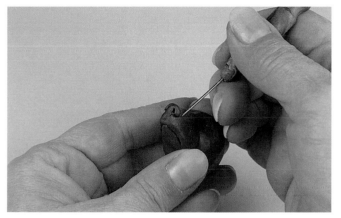

10

Finish the U-shape by drawing the small tapestry needle down and around to the side of the nose. Use the diagonal groove on the side of the nose as your guide.

11 THE EYES AND LIDS

Use the rod method to measure a small amount of Black clay to make ⅛" (0.3cm) diameter eyeballs. Bake for twenty minutes at 275° F. Press the eyeballs into the clay just below the top of the muzzle, on a line above the corners of the mouth. Shape the eyelids from very small, slightly flattened rods of clay. Shape the lower lids first, then the upper lids. A ball of clay a little larger than ⅛" (0.3cm) in diameter is more than enough to create the eyelids for both eyes. Press in place with a large knitting needle.

TIP

If you find making very small eyeballs that are perfect every time tedious, use ball bearings or round glass beads.

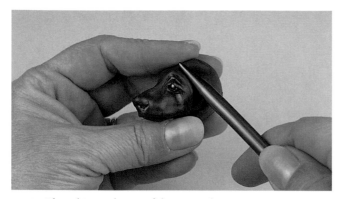

12 The orbits, or bones of the eye sockets, are a prominent feature. Pivot the shaft of a large knitting needle around the outside of the eyes and the brows to accent them.

13 **SHAPING THE BODY ARMATURE**
Making the body armature in stages gives you more control over the final shape. Fold a 2' (61cm) sheet of foil lengthwise, making it 2' long × 6" wide (61cm × 15.2cm). Gather together and twist tightly, forming a foil rod a little less than 5" (12.7cm) long.

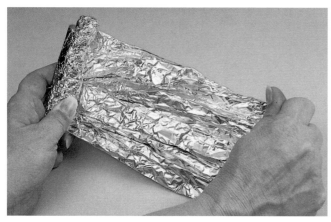

14 Gather a 12" (30.5cm) sheet of foil until it measures 6" × 12" (15.2cm × 30.5cm) and wrap tightly around the center of the twisted rod.

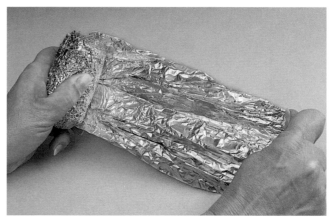

15 Wrap the rod again with three additional sheets of gathered foil. Each sheet should be 12" (30.5cm) square, gathered to 6" (15.2cm) width.

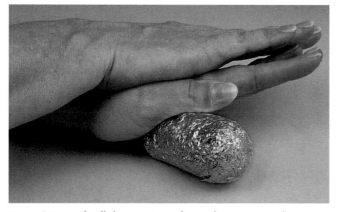

16 Press and roll the armature after each wrapping. The core should match the size and shape of the body armature diagram on page 47.

TIP

After you've covered the armature with clay, use the palm of your hand to rub the bear's body smooth. Do the same after you've built up the rump, belly and neck—imperfections caused by anxious fingers will disappear. This project teaches you how to control larger amounts of clay; keeping it smooth is a necessary skill.

17 BUILDING UP THE BODY

Use 1½ balls of clay to plaster the body armature (A) with small pieces. Rub smooth. Use 2½ balls to make an oval pancake ⅛" (0.3cm) thick. Stretch and wrap around the body. Blend the seams and rub smooth with the palm of your hand (B).

Applying the next three appliqués before you blend them will help you position them correctly. Build up the rump with an egg-shaped disk made of a full ball. Shape the belly with an oval strap 2¾" long × 1½" wide (7cm × 3.8cm) made from a full ball. Roll two full balls together and flatten to a ½" (1.3cm) thick disk for the neck (C). Blend the rump appliqué first and the neck last (D).

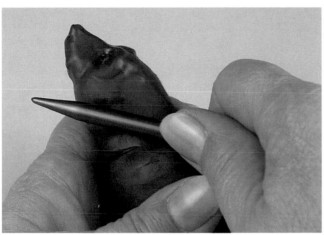

18 ATTACHING THE HEAD

Position the head on the neck and blend the seams. At this point the head looks too small for the neck. The next step will correct this.

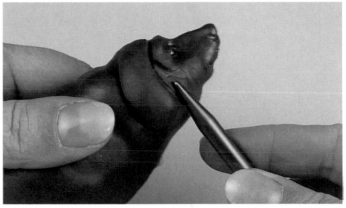

19 BUILDING UP THE JOWLS AND CROWN

Add slightly flattened rods to each side of the head. Use a quarter ball for each. Take care around the eye sockets when you blend the seams. Reshape them if necessary. Finish shaping the jowls by stroking them toward the back.

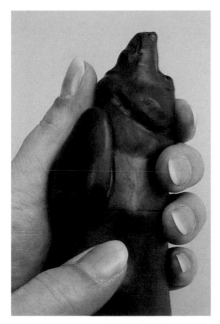

20 BUILDING UP THE CHEST

Make an egg-shaped disk from half a ball. Apply it to the chest and blend the seams.

21 MODELING THE NECK

Press two or three folds in the neck with a medium knitting needle. You can use the texture diagram on page 54 as a guide.

22 THE EARS

The bear's ears are surprisingly thin and need support. Copy the ear pattern on page 47 onto card stock stiffened with cyanoacrylic glue. Cut out two ears. Coat both sides of the armatures with vinyl glue and let dry. Curl the armatures (A), then fold a thin sheet of clay over each (B). Pinch firmly to make the clay adhere to the armature. Tear off the excess clay and rub the ears smooth (C). ¹⁄₁₆ of a ball of clay is more than enough to cover each armature.

23
Position the ears directly behind and as far back from the eyes as the eyes are from the tip of the nose. Drawing a deep groove in the clay that matches the curve of the ears makes it easier to insert the ears.

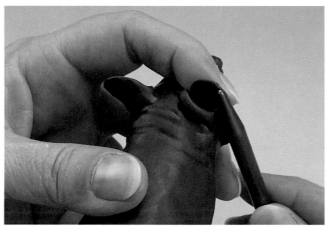

24
Support the back of the ear with a ¾" (1.9cm) long rod of clay made from ¹⁄₃₂ of a ball. Wrap the rod around the base of the ear.

25
To shape the inside of the ear, push a large knitting needle into the clay inside the ear and move it from side to side. Support the back of the ear with your finger during this step.

26 SHAPING THE LEGS AND FEET

The front and hind legs and feet are similar in appearance. You'll use the same technique to shape them, but different amounts of clay. Beginning with the front legs, form a slightly tapered cylinder from 1½ balls of clay. It should be 2" (5.1cm) long (A). Roll the cylinder gently between your fingers ¾" (1.9cm) from the tapered end to shape a club (B). Press the large end against the work surface to form a flat stump (C). Then flatten the small end and bend the leg forward (D).

Use 1¾ balls for the hind legs and roll to form a tapered cylinder 2½" (6.4cm) long. Roll the cylinder 1" (2.5cm) from the tapered end to form a club. Shape the stump and foot as you did for the front legs.

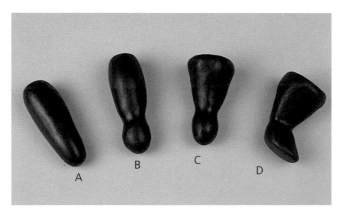

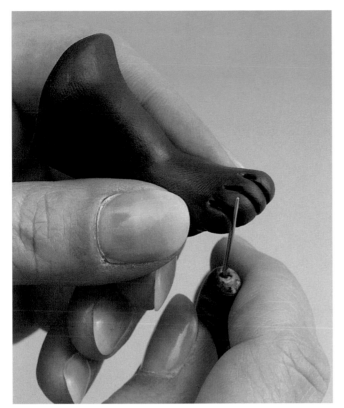

27 There are five toes on each foot, but the thumbs are often hidden. Mark four toes on the front foot and fives toes on the hind foot with a small tapestry needle. Widen the cleft between each toe with a small knitting needle.

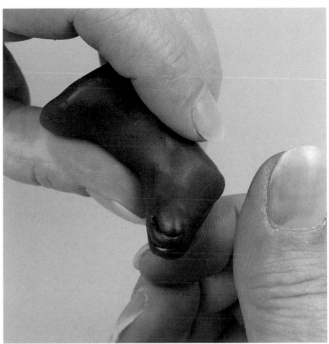

28 Press a large knitting needle against the outside of each foot to define the shape of the outer toes.

29 Press your finger on the side of each foot to shape a slight curve and arch, then pinch to the back to form a heel. Take care not to shape four left feet during this step.

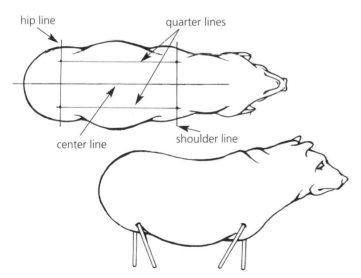

hip line

quarter lines

center line

shoulder line

30 ATTACHING THE LEGS

The front legs attach to the body halfway between the base of the neck and the pit of the chest, where the belly begins. The hind legs attach ⅓ of the way between the base of the belly and the rear. These are the shoulder and hip lines. Lightly draw them on the base of your sculpture.

Mark the center line of the body. Mark a line on each side of the center line, halfway between the center line and the sides of the belly where the body is widest. These are the quarter lines.

Pierce the body and foil core where the quarter lines cross the shoulder and hip lines. If you want your bear to look as if he's walking, pierce the body at the angles shown. Use a needle the same diameter as the metal bones. Insert the bones.

TIP

Even with a tightly packed foil armature, wire bones can shift. A drop of Super Glue deep in the "socket" will hold those bones in place.

31 Pierce each leg in the center and thread onto the bone. Push the stump against the body and blend the seams. Attaching the legs in pairs helps to pose them properly. Blend each pair before attaching the second pair.

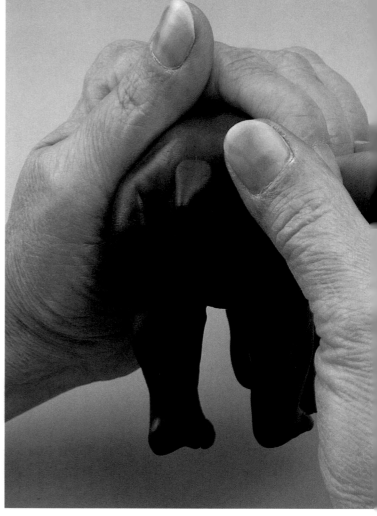

32 THE SHOULDERS AND THIGHS
Apply an oval disk made from a half ball of clay to build up the shoulder. Blend the seams. Build up the thigh with flat ovals each made from 1¼ balls. Blend the seams.

33 THE TAIL
Shape a small egg from ¹⁄₁₆ of a ball. Attach to the rump and blend the upper seam.

TEXTURE PATTERNS
The bear's fur is like that of the mouse, the cottontail or the seal. From nose to tail, it follows the line of the body and grows parallel to the bones. On the belly it radiates toward the navel.

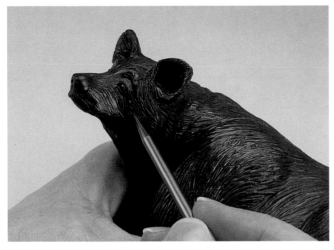

34 TEXTURING THE BEAR

Start texturing the bear in those hard to reach areas—the belly, the insides of the legs and the feet. Work your way up the body using overlapping strokes. Texture lightly on the muzzle, but use a heavier touch on the rest of the bear, especially where there are folds in the skin and fur. A medium knitting needle is the most effective tool for texturing the black bear. When finished, bake the bear in a glass pan at 275° F for two hours.

35 THE DRY BRUSH COAT

Blend a creamy gold from Titanium White and Raw Sienna and dry brush the insides of the ears, the muzzle, chin and brows. Let dry and paint the muzzle and chin with a second dry-brush coat.

36 THE WASH AND DETAIL COATS

Paint all but the dry brushed areas with a Black wash. The wash should be fairly thick, but not opaque; you want the warmth of the brown clay to shine through. Apply a thin Black wash on the dry brushed areas—the muzzle, brows, chin and inner ears. Let it flow into the texture lines on the muzzle and around the eyes. When the wash coat is dry, use a no. 00 brush to paint the nose, eyes and upper lip Black. Let dry, then make the eyes shine with a bit of gloss varnish.

The Basset Hound

There is no better dog for long walks in the woods or along the shore. Steady, inquisitive and deliberate, the basset is a finder of things. With a basset at my side, I have always found the best route up rocky cliffs or through scrubby brush—with such short legs, the easy path was the only path. My basset's keen nose has led me to nests of cottontails, beaver dams and a badger's set. With her at my side, I've seen a new-born fawn and sat next to coyote. Give a basset the lead and you'll find wonders.

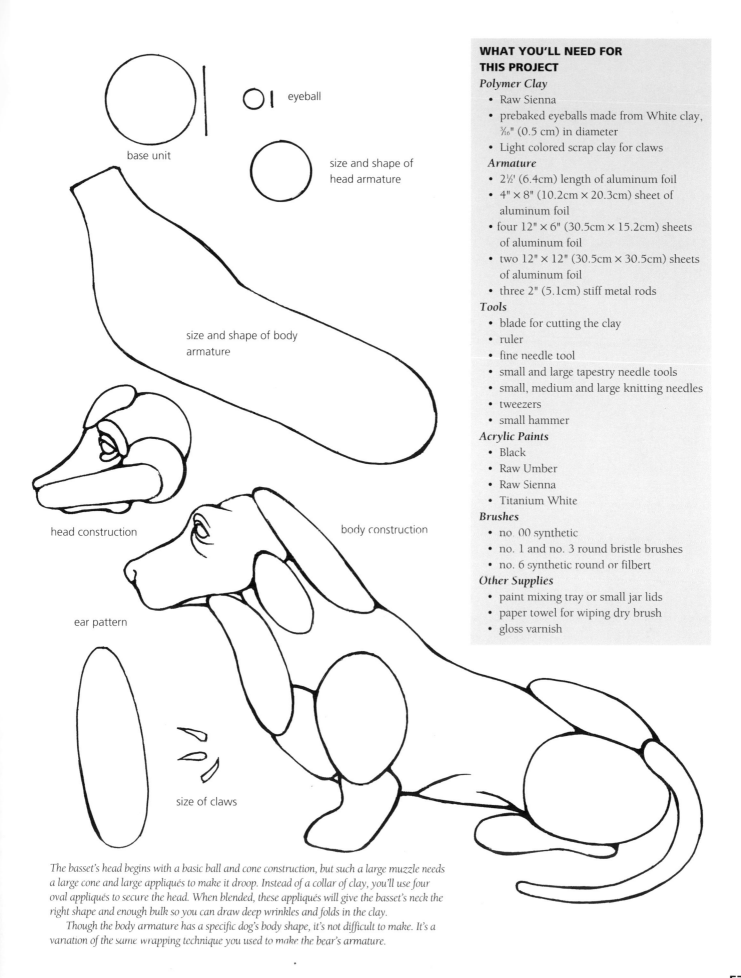

base unit

eyeball

size and shape of head armature

size and shape of body armature

head construction

body construction

ear pattern

size of claws

WHAT YOU'LL NEED FOR THIS PROJECT

Polymer Clay
- Raw Sienna
- prebaked eyeballs made from White clay, ³⁄₁₆" (0.5 cm) in diameter
- Light colored scrap clay for claws

Armature
- 2½' (6.4cm) length of aluminum foil
- 4" × 8" (10.2cm × 20.3cm) sheet of aluminum foil
- four 12" × 6" (30.5cm × 15.2cm) sheets of aluminum foil
- two 12" × 12" (30.5cm × 30.5cm) sheets of aluminum foil
- three 2" (5.1cm) stiff metal rods

Tools
- blade for cutting the clay
- ruler
- fine needle tool
- small and large tapestry needle tools
- small, medium and large knitting needles
- tweezers
- small hammer

Acrylic Paints
- Black
- Raw Umber
- Raw Sienna
- Titanium White

Brushes
- no. 00 synthetic
- no. 1 and no. 3 round bristle brushes
- no. 6 synthetic round or filbert

Other Supplies
- paint mixing tray or small jar lids
- paper towel for wiping dry brush
- gloss varnish

The basset's head begins with a basic ball and cone construction, but such a large muzzle needs a large cone and large appliqués to make it droop. Instead of a collar of clay, you'll use four oval appliqués to secure the head. When blended, these appliqués will give the basset's neck the right shape and enough bulk so you can draw deep wrinkles and folds in the clay.

Though the body armature has a specific dog's body shape, it's not difficult to make. It's a variation of the same wrapping technique you used to make the bear's armature.

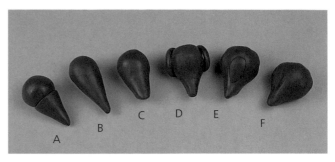

1 MEASURING THE CLAY

You'll need three two-ounce (56.7g) packages of Raw Sienna Clay. Divide each package into twelve sections, then combine two sections to find the base unit, a ball of clay a little smaller than 1" (2.5cm) in diameter. This project uses a little less than nineteen balls of clay.

2 BUILDING A BASIC HEAD

Use a 4" × 8" (10.2 cm × 20.3cm) sheet of foil to make a round foil core. Cover the core with a disk made of ¾ of a ball. Use half of a ball to make a 1¼" (3.2cm) long cone. Attach the cone (A) and blend the seams (B), then snub the tip with your finger (C). Use ¼ of a ball for each cheek (D). To build the profile, form a teardrop from ¹⁄₁₆ of a ball and flatten. Center on top of the head (E) and blend (F).

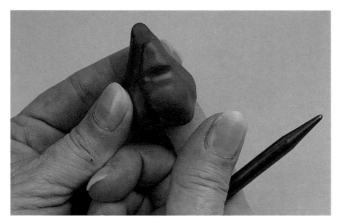

3 THE LOWER JAW AND MOUTH

Roll an egg from ⅛ of a ball of clay. Flatten it and apply it to the base of the muzzle. Press a groove across the middle. This forms the "hinge" of the jaw and divides the mouth from the base of the lower jaw. Blend the hinge and the base of the jaw, but not the mouth.

4

Shape two 1½" (3.8cm) long strips and apply to each side of the muzzle. Use a quarter ball for each strip. Blend the top seams, but not the bottom. Stroke down gently to create a drooping muzzle. Use a small tapestry needle to redraw the cleft lip if necessary.

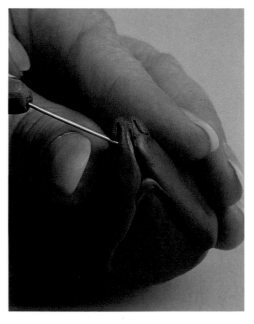

6 MARKING THE NOSE

The basset's nostrils have the same U-shaped cleft as the black bear (page 49). Use the same technique. Begin by pressing an angled groove on the sides of the nose with a knitting needle, then use a small tapestry needle to mark the nostrils.

5

Define the lower lip and widen the base of the jaw with a large knitting needle.

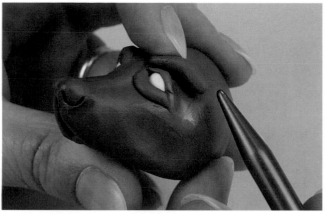
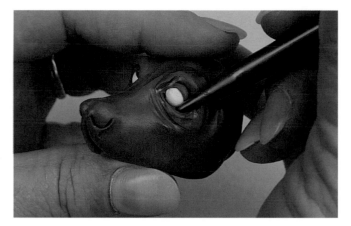

7 THE EYES, LIDS AND BROWS

Use the rod method to measure a small amount of White clay for ³⁄₁₆" (0.5cm) diameter eyeballs. Bake the eyeballs for twenty minutes at 275° F. Position the eyeballs halfway between the tip of the nose and the back of the head. Make a thin strip for the upper eyelid from a ⅛" (0.3cm) diameter ball of clay and apply. Make the lower lid from rods made of ¹⁄₆₄ of a ball each. Apply and blend. Build up the brows with tapered rods placed just above the upper lid and blend. Use ¹⁄₃₂ of a ball for each brow.

8 SHAPING THE BODY ARMATURE

Fold a 2½' × 1' (76cm × 30cm) sheet of foil, making it 2½' × 6" (76cm × 15.2cm). Gather, then twist tightly to form a cylinder 5" to 6" (12.7cm to 15.2cm) long. Bend 1½" (3.8cm) from one end to form the neck.

9

Build up the body with two sheets of foil, each 2' × 6" (76cm × 15.2cm). Gather each, making them 4" × 6" (10.2cm × 15.2cm). One at a time, wrap them around the body, but not the neck. After each wrap, roll the core on a table top to shape.

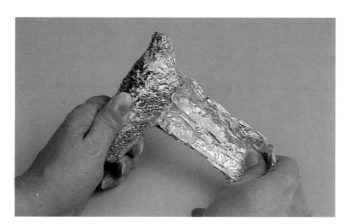

10

Build up the ribcage with a 12" (30.5cm) square sheet of foil, gathered to 12" × 2" (30.5cm × 5.1cm) Wrap tightly around the body near the neck and press firmly into shape.

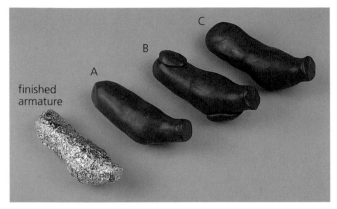

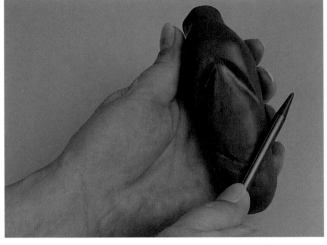

11 BUILDING UP THE BODY

Use two balls of clay to plaster the body armature with small pieces. Rub smooth. Use 3¾ balls to make an oval pancake ⅛" (0.3cm) thick. Stretch and wrap around the body. Blend the seams and rub smooth (A). Apply an oval disk made of a half ball to the rump and an oval disk made of a full ball to build up the chest (B). Blend the seams (C).

12

Use the shaft of a large knitting needle to press four grooves that define the belly. Rub these grooves smooth with your fingers.

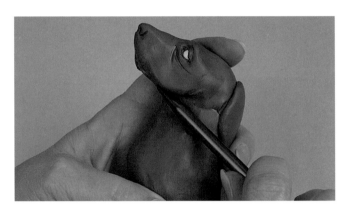

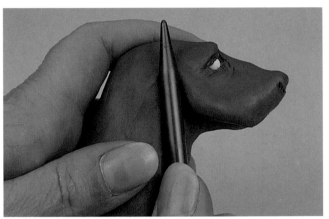

13 ATTACHING THE HEAD AND MODELING THE NECK

Position the head on the neck and secure by working clay from the neck onto the head. Four oval appliqués help to shape the neck. Use a half ball for the front and back of the neck and a quarter ball for each side. Apply the front and back appliqués. Blend the seams, using a large knitting needle as a roller. Apply the side appliqués, then blend, taking care around the mouth.

14 DEFINING THE JAW

Use the shaft of the large knitting needle to define the jawbone halfway between the eyes and the back of the head.

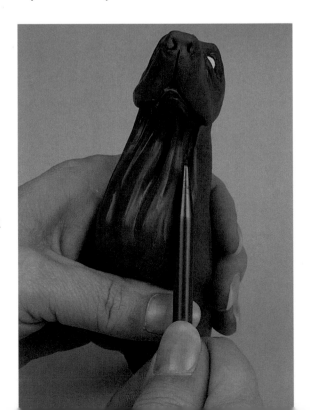

15 FOLDS IN THE NECK

Use a large knitting needle to press five deep folds on the front of the neck and chest. Beginning with the deepest, center fold, stroke down toward the chest, then up toward the mouth. Stroke the outermost folds next, beginning at the jaw line and stroking down. Draw folds halfway between the center and outermost folds, stroking down from the corners of the mouth. Finish by tilting and turning the head to pose.

TIP

This project teaches you how to control large amounts of clay. It also teaches you to use the thickness of the clay to your advantage.

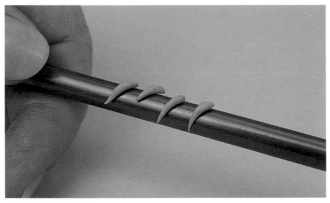

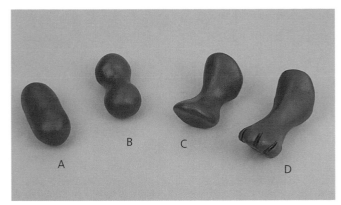

16 MAKING THE CLAWS

Use a light-colored clay for the claws. You will need eighteen. A ⅛" (0.3cm) ball of clay will make two claws. Roll small cones, then gently press them on the shaft of a knitting needle to curve them. Bake at 275° F for no less than twenty minutes. If you don't bake them long enough, they won't be strong enough.

17 THE FRONT LEGS AND PAWS

Use a half ball of clay for each front leg. Form a cylinder (A) about 1" (2.5cm) long and roll between your fingers to shape a barbell (B). Press the bell ends against the work surface to flatten (C). The basset's front feet have four clawed toes and a thumb-like "dew claw." Mark four toes by pressing into the clay with a small tapestry needle, then widen with a small knitting needle. Press a large knitting needle against the outside of each foot to define the shape of the outer toes (D).

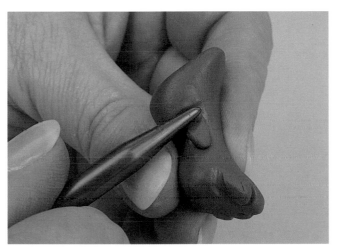

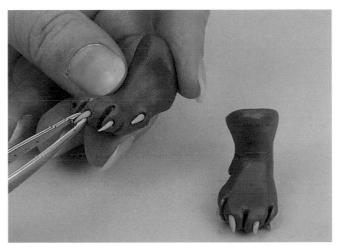

18 THE DEW CLAW

Shape the dew claw using a ⅛" (0.3cm) diameter ball of clay and blend.

19

Pierce each toe with a small knitting needle and use tweezers to insert the prebaked claws. Gently pinch the toes together to shape the foot.

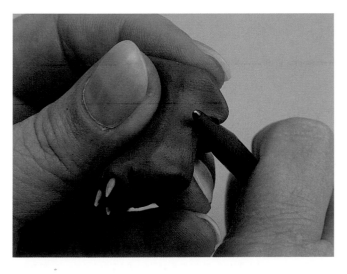

20

Pinch the back of each leg, then press up with a large knitting needle to form a pad called the "carpal cushion."

21 ATTACHING THE FRONT LEGS

To find out where to insert the bones, use the same method you used when you attached the bear's legs (pages 53-54). Mark the center line, the quarter lines and the shoulder line. To find out where to draw the quarter lines, use the widest point of the body. On the basset, this is at the shoulders. Pierce the body and foil core where the quarter and shoulder lines cross. Insert 1½" (3.8cm) long bones, then pierce each leg and thread onto the "bones." Secure the legs by working clay from the leg onto the body.

22 MODELING THE SHOULDERS

Use an oval disk made from a half ball of clay to build up each shoulder. Position on the body and blend the seams.

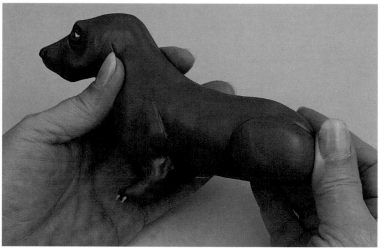

23 Use the knitting needle to outline the contours of the shoulders.

24 THE HIND LEGS AND FEET

Use 1¼ balls for each thigh. Flatten to form an oval and attach. Blend only where the thigh meets the rump.

25 THE HIND FEET

Use ¾ of a ball of clay for each foot. Roll to form an extended egg (A) and flatten the large end (B). Mark four toes with a large tapestry needle (C) and widen the cleft with a small knitting needle (D). Pierce the toes and insert the claws, then gently pinch the toes together (E).

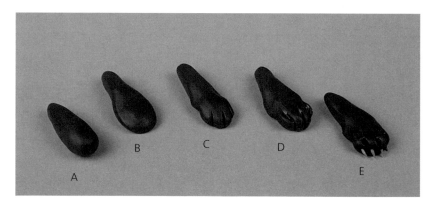

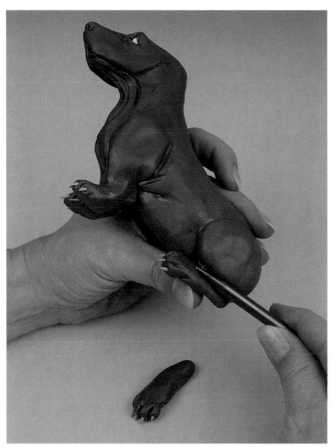

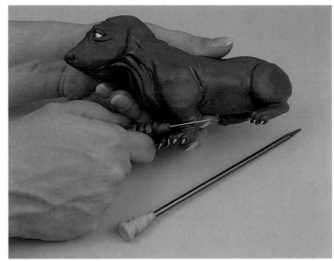

27 THE WRINKLES AND FOLDS

Use the shaft of the tapestry needle to wrinkle the front paws. Use the shaft of a medium knitting needle to press wrinkles across the neck and upper back.

26 Attach the feet at the base of the thigh and blend with the shaft of a large knitting needle.

28 TEXTURING THE BASSET HOUND

It's far easier to create the basset hound's texture if there are no ears and tail to get in the way. Use a small tapestry needle to create a sleek texture. Mark the belly button as a starting point and texture those hard to reach areas first—the belly, legs, neck and jaw. Next, texture the head, then work your way back and down the body. Don't forget the whisker follicles.

TEXTURE PATTERNS

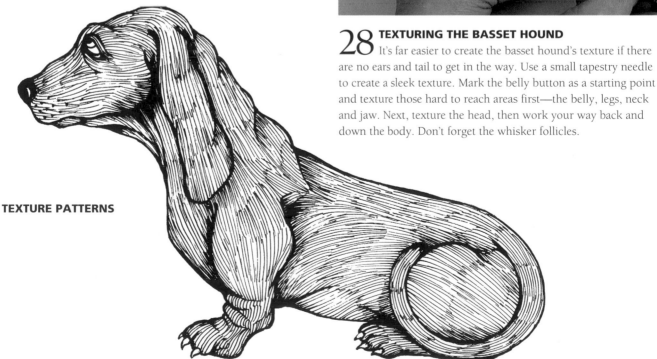

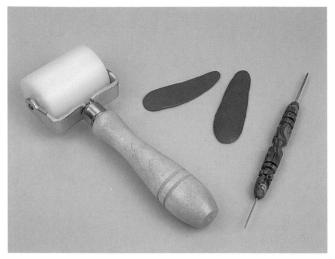

29 THE EARS

Use ⅛ of a ball (half of ¼) for each ear. Shape an extended egg and press flat, then use a roller to make the ears smooth and even. They should be a little longer than the head. Texture the ears on a flat surface before attaching them to the head.

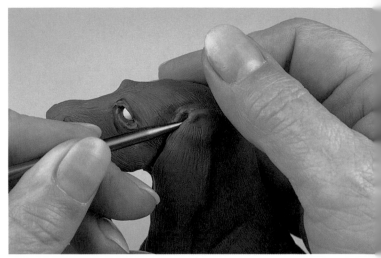

30

Curl the ears by laying them lengthwise over a large knitting needle. Attach them to the head and blend the seams. Use a medium knitting needle to gently lift the ears where they attach. Gently press them against the body, then retexture any smudged lines.

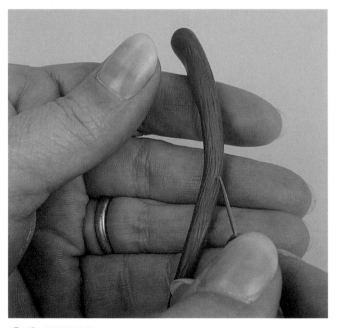

31 THE TAIL

Use a quarter of a ball of clay to shape the tail. Roll a tapered rod half as long as the body. Texture with a tapestry needle.

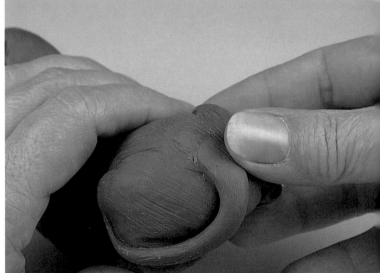

32

Press the base of the tail against the rump and blend the seams. Position the tail against the body. Redraw any smudged texture lines. Slightly deeper strokes on the tip of the tail will help secure it and give it a tufted appearance. Bake the basset at 275° F for two hours.

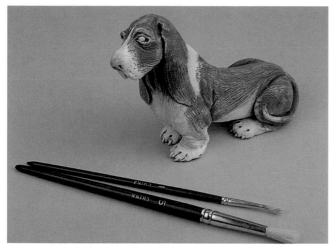

33 PAINTING THE WHITE COAT

Begin with a white dry brush coat, lightly painting the entire sculpture. After this coat is dry, paint the muzzle, chest, belly, legs, feet and the tip of the tail Titanium White. If you imagine the basset wearing socks, mittens and a long apron that hangs around his neck, the pattern is easy to follow. Use a no. 00 brush to paint a center line from the nose to the top of his head. Let dry.

34 THE BROWN COAT

Paint all but the white areas with a blend of Raw Umber and Raw Sienna. When dry, apply a very watery umber wash to every surface but the eyeballs. This stain should flow into the folds and leave only the slightest hint of color on the white coat.

35 THE BLACK COAT

Use a black stain to paint the saddle on his back. Also paint his nose black at this time.

MARKINGS

Bassets may be black with some golden-brown and white markings, or they can be russet or golden-brown with almost no markings. This is a tricolor basset, with its typically white chest, belly, legs and feet. The white muzzle with the central stripe is common to the tricolor, as is the black saddle. A white saddle with black "ticks" or spots is another common pattern.

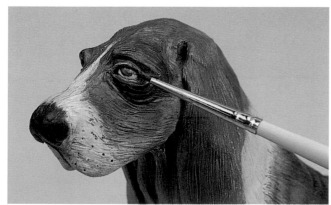

36 PAINTING THE EYES

Use a small brush to paint a Raw Umber iris. Because of the drooping lid, the iris is basically a half circle. Fill the center of the iris with Raw Sienna and let dry.

37

Paint a black pupil inside the iris. Use the no. 00 brush to outline the eyes with a black stain. When everything is dry, varnish the eyeballs with gloss varnish.

The White-Tailed Fawn

As we have cleared away our woodlands, leaving only small preserves and copses, we have also favored the white-tailed deer. Now, these delicate-seeming creatures are the most successful and abundant hoofed animal in all of North America, and we are its only true predator. Scout the edge of a lake or stream at dawn or dusk for your best chance of seeing a deer. Go quietly; they are as cautious as they are beautiful.

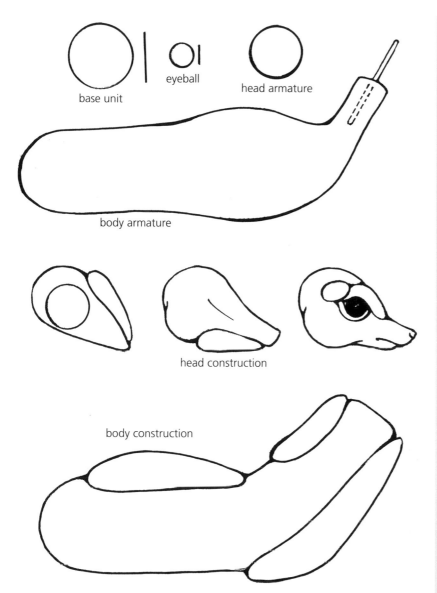

base unit

eyeball

head armature

body armature

head construction

body construction

The white-tailed fawn's body armature is a smaller, simpler version of the dog's body armature. Securing the head with a stiff wire is a necessary step. The head follows a very basic plan, combining techniques you already know, but you'll need to build up the brow with overlapping appliqués to model the fawn's large, wide-set eyes. To model the characteristic straight spine, you'll place an appliqué on the center back, not on the rump.

WHAT YOU'LL NEED FOR THIS PROJECT

Polymer Clay
- Raw Sienna
- prebaked eyeballs made from Black clay, ¼" (0.6 cm) in diameter

Armature
- 4" × 8" (10.2cm × 20.3cm) sheet of aluminum foil
- two 18" × 12" (45.7cm × 30.5cm) sheets of aluminum foil
- 12" × 6" (30.5cm × 15.2cm) sheet of aluminum foil
- 1" (2.5cm) metal rod
- two 3¼" (8.3cm) metal rods
- two 3½" (8.9cm) metal rods
- card stock stiffened with Super Glue

Tools
- blade for cutting the clay
- ruler
- fine needle tool
- small and large tapestry needle tools
- small, medium and large knitting needles
- needle-nose pliers or wire cutters

Acrylic Paints
- Black
- Raw Sienna
- Raw Umber
- Titanium White

Brushes
- no. 00 synthetic
- no. 1 and no. 3 round bristle brushes
- no. 6 synthetic round or filbert

Other Supplies
- paint mixing tray or four small jar lids
- paper towel for wiping dry brush
- vinyl glue (Sobo, Gem Tac or Aleene's Tacky)
- marking pen
- gloss varnish

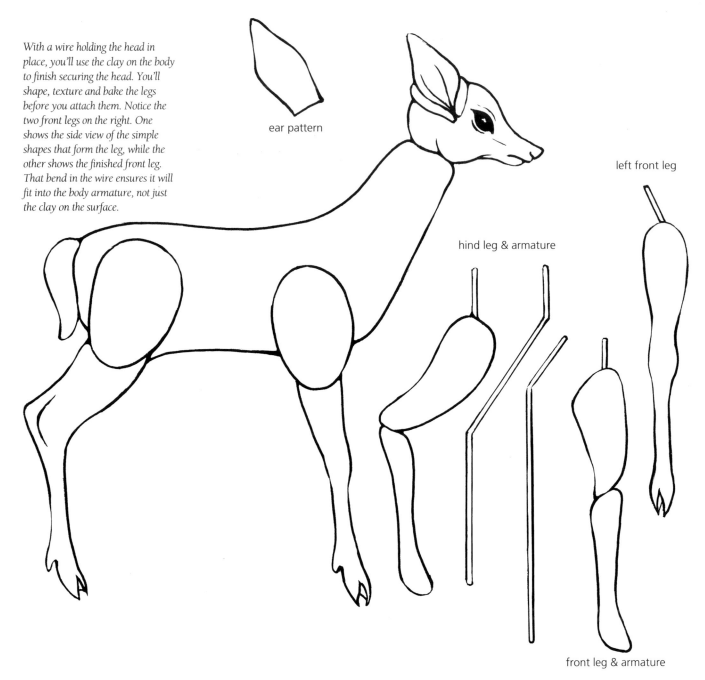

With a wire holding the head in place, you'll use the clay on the body to finish securing the head. You'll shape, texture and bake the legs before you attach them. Notice the two front legs on the right. One shows the side view of the simple shapes that form the leg, while the other shows the finished front leg. That bend in the wire ensures it will fit into the body armature, not just the clay on the surface.

ear pattern

left front leg

hind leg & armature

front leg & armature

1 MEASURING THE CLAY You'll need two two-ounce (56.7g) packages of Raw Sienna clay. Divide each package into twelve sections. Roll into balls a little smaller than ¾" (1.9cm) in diameter. This project uses a little less than twenty balls of clay.

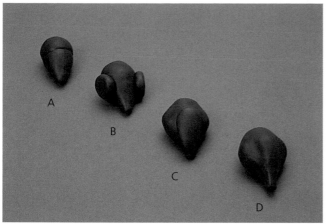

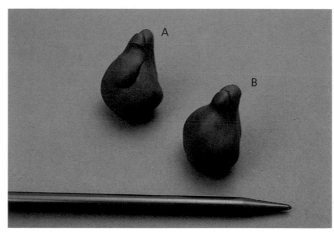

2 BUILDING A BASIC HEAD

Use a 4" × 8" (10.2cm × 20.3cm) sheet of foil to make a round foil core. Cover the core with a disk made of half a ball. Attach a cone made of half a ball (A). Blend the seams. Shape two disks, each from a quarter ball, and apply to the sides of the head, halfway between the tip of the nose and the back of the head (B). Blend the seams. To build the profile, form an extended egg from a quarter of a ball. Flatten and apply it so the small end of this appliqué begins at the tip of the nose (C). Notice how adding these appliqués helps to form the eye sockets (D).

3 THE LOWER JAW AND MOUTH

Shape the lower jaw with a flattened egg made from 1/16 of a ball of clay. Apply to the base of the muzzle and press a groove across the midpoint. Accent the corners of the mouth, then blend the clay at the base of the jaw.

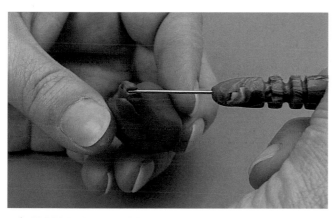

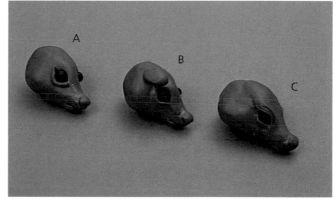

4 MARKING THE NOSE

Press an angled groove on each side of the nose with a knitting needle. Press a slight **V** on the top of the nose. The nostrils have a comma shape. Press the point of a small tapestry needle into the clay at a slight angle to make this shape.

5 THE EYES AND LIDS

Use the rod method to measure a small amount of Black clay for 1/4" (0.6cm) diameter eyeballs. Bake for twenty minutes at 275° F. Position the eyeballs halfway between the tip of the nose and the back of the head. Divide 1/8 of a ball into quarters. Shape one of these quarters into a thin rod for the lower lid and set just below the eye (A). Combine the remaining three quarters into a ball and cut in half. Shape half of the ball into a strip and the other half into a tiny oval disk. Apply the strip above the eye to begin shaping the upper lid. Lay the tiny oval on top of the strip just behind the eye (B). Blend the seams carefully (C). Repeat for the other eye.

TIP

If your sculpture doesn't look quite right and you can't figure out why, hold it up to a mirror and study the reflection. Small mistakes such as offset eyes or an uneven jaw will be more obvious.

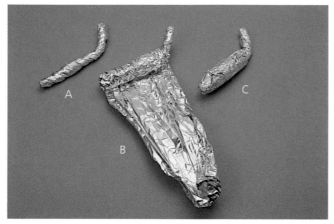

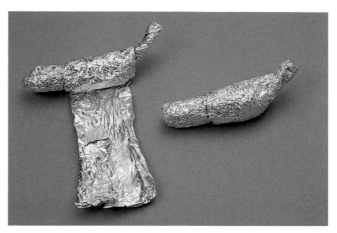

6 SHAPING THE BODY ARMATURE

Fold a 1½' × 1' (3.8cm × 30cm) sheet of foil, making it 1½' × 6" (16cm × 15.2cm). Gather, then twist tightly to form a cylinder 5" to 6" (12.7cm to 15.2cm) long. Bend 1½" (3.8cm) from one end to form the neck (A). Gather a 1' × 1½' (30cm × 46cm) sheet of foil to 4" wide × 1½' (10.2cm × 46cm). Wrap tightly around the core (B) and roll firmly against a table top to shape (C).

7

Build up the ribcage and shoulder blades with a 12" × 6" (30.5cm × 15.2cm) square sheet of foil gathered to 12" × 2" (30.5cm × 5.1cm). Wrap tightly around the body near the neck and press firmly into shape.

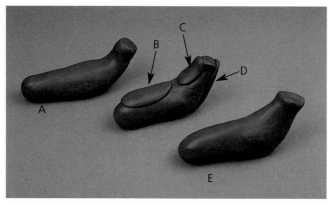

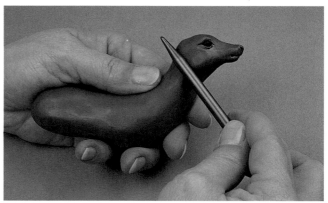

8 BUILDING UP THE BODY

Use two balls of clay to plaster the body armature with small pieces and rub smooth. Use 2½ balls to make an oval pancake ⅛" (0.3cm) thick. Stretch and wrap around the body. Blend the seams and rub smooth (A). Apply an oval disk made of a full ball to the center back (B). Thicken the nape of the neck with an oval disk made of a half ball (C). Build up the chest and neck with an elongated oval disk made of 1¼ balls (D). Apply and blend these pieces one at a time (E).

9 ATTACHING THE HEAD AND MODELING THE NECK

Insert a stiff 1" (2.5cm) metal rod in the neck. Prepierce the base of the head and push it down onto the wire until it touches the body. Take care not to flatten the top of the head. Use a large knitting needle as a roller to blend the seams as you work clay from the neck onto the head. Reshape the jaw and the top and back of the head, if necessary.

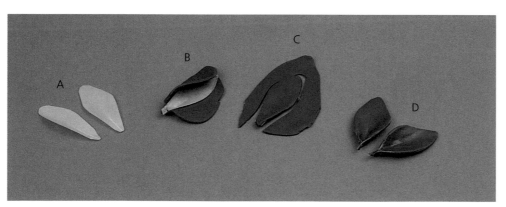

10 THE EARS

Trace the ear pattern and cut two ear armatures from glue-stiffened paper. Fold the base of each ear by pinching it. Coat the paper with vinyl glue (A). After the glue is dry, cover each armature with a thin sheet of clay made of ⅛ of a ball (B). Press firmly, then pinch or trim off the excess clay (C). Rub smooth (D).

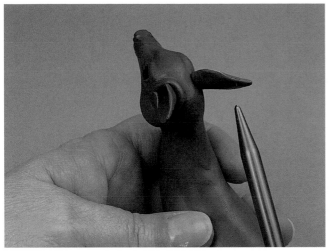

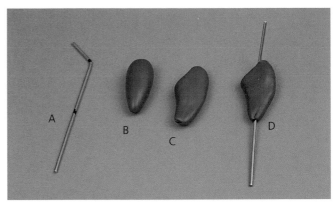

11 Pierce the ear sockets halfway between the eyes and the back of the head. Pinch the bases of the ears and insert them into the holes. Secure each ear with a rod of clay made from 1/16 of a ball. Wrap the rod all the way around the base of the ear and blend the seams.

12 THE UPPER SECTION OF THE FRONT LEGS
For each front leg, mark and bend a 3¼" (8.3cm) armature rod according to the pattern diagram on page 68. Coat the rods with vinyl glue and let dry (A). Shape ¾ of a ball into an elongated egg (B). Flatten slightly, then stroke to refine its shape (C). Prepierce the piece and thread it onto the rod, up to the bend. The bend in the wire should point away from the upper leg piece (this is shown more clearly in step 19). Stroke the clay to lengthen it until it fits between the marks on the wire (D). Let it rest to ensure a good bond between the glue and the clay.

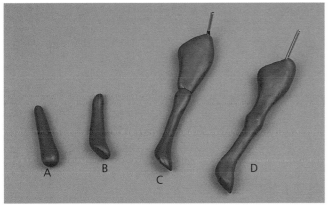

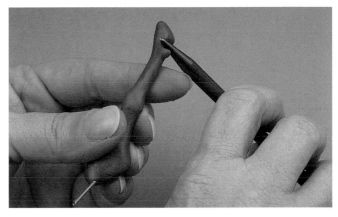

13 THE LOWER SECTION OF THE FRONT LEGS
Use half of a ball to shape a tapered rod (A). Flatten the large end at an angle to begin forming the hoof (B) and thread it onto the bone. Stretch and pinch the clay onto the rod until it meets the upper limb (C). Carefully blend the seams, then let the clay rest. Shape the "knee" by stroking the clay from just above the hoof toward the upper leg and from the upper leg toward the lower leg (D).

14 SHAPING THE HIND CLAWS
The white-tailed deer has a small pair of hind claws on each foot. To form the claws, pinch the back of the leg near the hoof, then push the clay up with a large knitting needle.

15 FINISHING THE HIND CLAWS
Use a small tapestry needle to split the hind claw. Use a medium knitting needle to refine the shape of the claws.

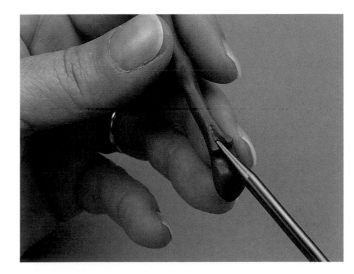

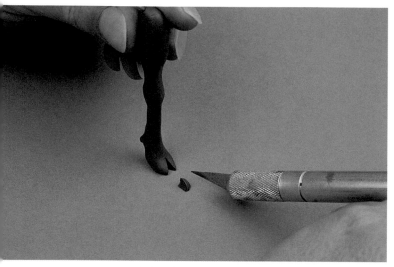

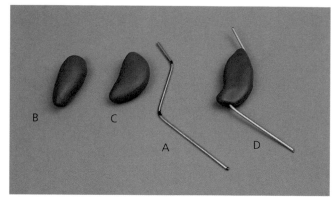

16 Caress the hoof to a point. Stand the leg upright and press it down gently on a flat surface to insure that the fawn will stand with his hooves flat on the ground. With the leg still held upright, cut a small **V** in the front of the hoof.

17 THE UPPER SECTION OF THE HIND LEGS

For each hind leg, mark and bend a 3½" (8.9cm) long rod according to the pattern diagram on page 68. Treat with vinyl glue and let dry (A). Roll 1¼ balls into an elongated egg 1" (2.5cm) long (B). Flatten the ball slightly, then curve and prepierce it (C). Thread the upper leg onto the rod as shown. Stroke and stretch the piece to fit inside the marks, then press firmly as you shape it (D). Let the thigh rest.

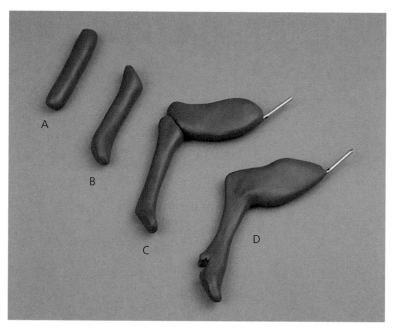

18 THE LOWER SECTION OF THE HIND LEGS

Use half a ball to shape the hind cannon (the area from the "knee" to the forelock). Roll the clay to form a rod (A), then flatten both ends at parallel angles (B). Thread the rod onto the bone, stretching the clay until it meets the thigh (C). Blend the seams, then stroke the clay from the hoof toward the thigh. Let the leg rest, then model the hind claws and split the hoof as you did for the front legs (D).

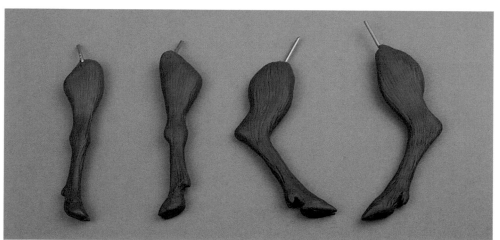

19 TEXTURING AND BAKING THE LEGS

Follow the texture pattern diagram on page 74 to completely texture all four legs. Bake for forty minutes at 275° F. Lay the legs on an index card to protect their texture and use a glass baking pan.

20 PLACING THE LEGS

Mark the quarter lines halfway between the center line and the widest point of the body, usually at the shoulders. Find the shoulder and hip lines by dividing the length of the body into thirds. The shoulder line crosses the center of the upper body. The hip line crosses the center of the lower body.

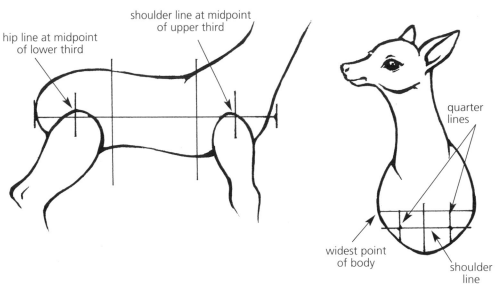

hip line at midpoint of lower third

shoulder line at midpoint of upper third

quarter lines

widest point of body

shoulder line

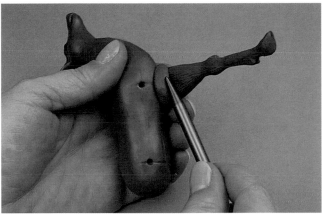

21 INSERTING AND SECURING THE LEGS

Pierce the body and foil core where the quarter lines cross the shoulder and hip lines. Pierce the shoulder sockets at an angle, matching the slight bend in the armature rod. Beginning with the front legs, insert and secure the legs in pairs. Push the rod into the socket until the upper limb presses firmly against the body and is seated in the clay. Secure the legs to the body on the inside and outside of each leg with rods of clay each made from ¼ a ball. Blend the seams. Don't worry about covering the texture; those grooves will help the unbaked clay adhere to the baked legs.

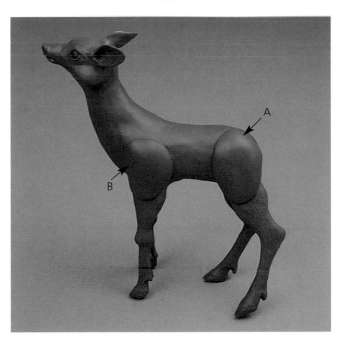

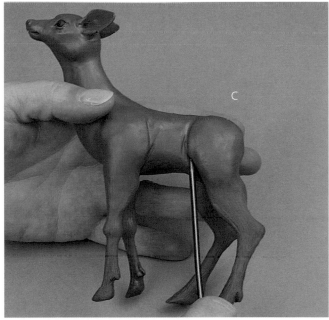

22 FINISHING THE LEGS

Stand the fawn upright and adjust the position of the legs, resealing any seams that crack. Build up each thigh with a flattened oval disk made from a full ball (A). Build up each shoulder with a flattened egg made from a half ball (B). Blend the seams and refine their shapes with a large knitting needle (C). Again, don't worry about covering up the texture on the legs.

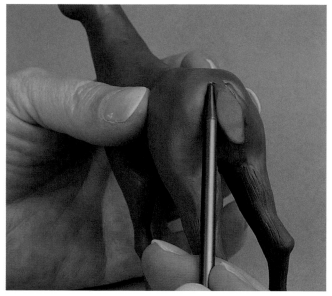

23 THE FLAG

Roll an egg from ⅛ of a ball. Caress each end to a point, then flatten slightly. Place on the rump and blend the seams. Use a medium knitting needle to refine the tail's diamond shape.

TEXTURE PATTERNS

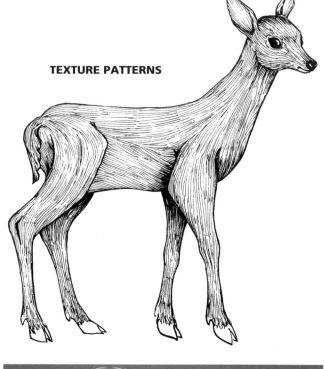

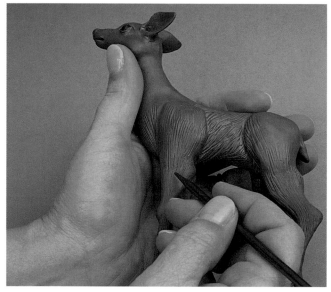

24 TEXTURING THE FAWN

Work on the hard-to-reach areas first (the belly, the insides of the legs, the neck and jaw), then work your way from the nose back down the body. Give the insides of the ears a downy texture. You'll find you have no trouble texturing the legs; your tool will glide from unbaked to baked clay easily and the texture lines will match.

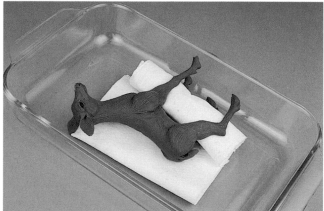

25 BAKING

Bake the fawn standing upright in a glass pan at 275° F for twenty minutes, just until the clay begins to cure. After twenty minutes, use a hot pad to lay the fawn down on a cushion of paper towels thick enough to raise the ear above the bottom of the pan. To prevent the legs from shifting, insert tightly rolled paper towels between them. Be careful not to burn your fingers—the deer will be very hot. Bake for forty more minutes at 275° F.

TIP

Polymer clay softens before it cures. Even when it is fully cured, it is still affected by heat. Those prebaked legs may be supported by stiff metal bones, but they are held in place by thin layers of clay in the shoulders and thighs, clay that will soften and compress slightly. As that clay compresses, a downward shift can place sudden stress on the legs. Standing the fawn upright for the first twenty minutes of baking insures a solid stance. Laying the fawn down for the rest of the baking time will protect the legs from stress fractures and prevent disaster.

26 DRY BRUSHING AND APPLYING THE WHITE DETAILS

Begin with a white dry brush coat over the entire fawn. Next, paint the belly, chest, inner legs and sides of the tail with more white. Paint the lower jaw with white to resemble a beard. The insides of the ears are white, too. Paint the camouflage spots on the back following the pattern in the next illustration.

27 Paint one row of uniform spots, resembling a dashed line, on each side of the deer, running from the tail along the edge of the back and halfway up the neck. Below the dashed line, the fawn's sides are covered with camouflage spots loosely arranged in rows that follow the line of the body. These spots are irregularly shaped and no two are alike.

TIP

To give the fawn a downy look, repeat the dry brush, staining and brightening coats. Use a soft synthetic or sable brush for the additional dry brush coat. Though this technique is bad for the brush and can ruin it, the results are remarkably soft.

28 THE WASH AND LAST DETAILS

After the white paint dries, apply a staining wash of Raw Sienna mixed with Raw Umber to the entire sculpture. Darken the top of the muzzle and let it dry. Brighten the white belly, beard, tail and inner ears with white. Touch up the camouflage spots and use a dry brush to paint the upper eyelids white. When dry, paint the nose, eyes and hooves black. Varnish the eyes with gloss varnish.

The Red Fox

You may have seen the trail of the red fox—narrow, dog-like tracks running in a straight line across wintry fields, along fence lines, at the forest's edge or in our city parks. Unlike our well-bred pet dogs who leave ambling trails, the fox moves with efficiency and deliberation. A nighttime hunter, the country fox dispatches rats, mice, birds and earthworms with relish, but will also eat corn, sweet grasses and berries. Intelligent and adaptable, the city fox has developed a taste for the scraps we throw away.

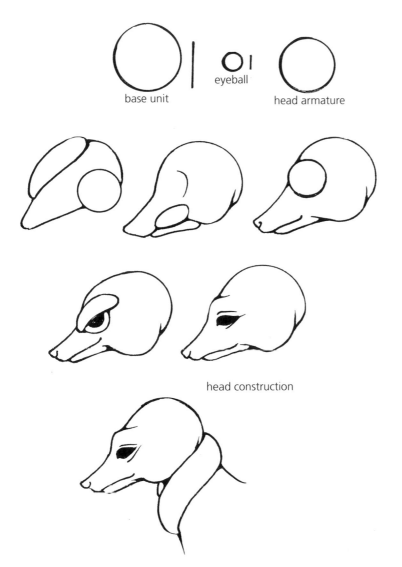

base unit

eyeball

head armature

head construction

The red fox's head is one of the most complex heads in this book, yet the shapes are still very basic: a ball and cone built up with simple profile and cheek appliqués. Pinching the muzzle makes it narrower and sharper, the same technique you used with the black bear. Small, egg-shaped pieces widen the upper jaw, while a flattened egg builds the lower jaw. Disks build up the eye sockets and help to form the forehead. The brows and lids are similar to the fawn's.

WHAT YOU'LL NEED FOR THIS PROJECT

Polymer Clay
- Raw Sienna
- prebaked eyeballs made from Black clay, a little less than ³⁄₁₆" (0.5cm) in diameter

Armature
- 4" × 8" (10.2cm × 20.3cm) sheet of aluminum foil
- two 12" (30.5cm) square sheets of aluminum foil
- two 12" × 6" (30.5cm × 15.2cm) sheets of aluminum foil
- two 2¾" (7cm) metal rods
- two 2½" (6.4cm) metal rods
- 1½" (3.8cm) metal rod
- card stock stiffened with Super Glue

Tools
- blade for cutting the clay
- ruler
- fine needle tool
- small and large tapestry needle tools
- small, medium and large knitting needles
- needle-nose pliers or wire cutters

Acrylic Paints
- Black
- Burnt Umber
- Raw Sienna
- Titanium White

Brushes
- no. 00 synthetic
- no. 1 and no. 3 round bristle brushes
- no. 6 synthetic round or filbert

Other Supplies
- paint mixing tray or four small jar lids
- paper towel for wiping dry brush
- cyanoacrylate glue (Super Glue)
- vinyl glue (Sobo, Gem Tac or Aleene's Tacky)
- marking pen
- gloss varnish

1 MEASURING THE CLAY

You'll need three two-ounce (56.7g) packages of Raw Sienna clay. Divide each package into twelve balls of clay, each a little smaller than ¾" (1.9cm) in diameter. This project uses a little more than twenty balls of clay.

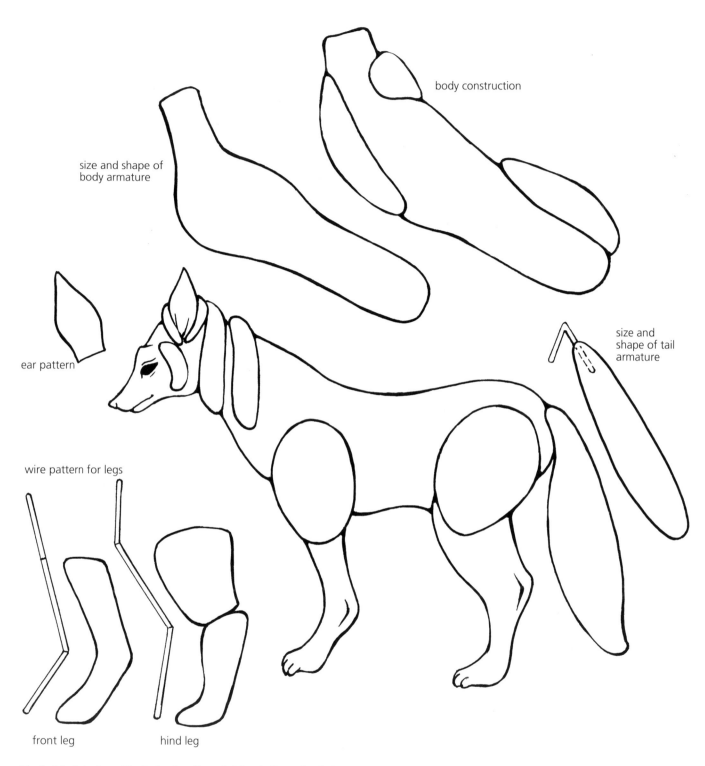

body construction

size and shape of
body armature

ear pattern

size and
shape of tail
armature

wire pattern for legs

front leg

hind leg

The fox's body is almost identical to the white-tailed fawn's. Except for obvi-
ous differences, the legs are also very similar to the fawn's. Using a foil core
in the tail reduces its weight, a technique just right for this animal.

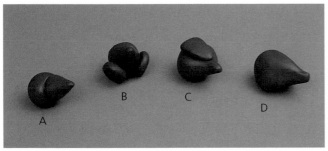

2 BUILDING A BASIC HEAD

Use a 4" × 8" (10.2cm × 20.3cm) sheet of foil to make a round foil core. Cover the core with a disk made of half a ball. Attach a cone made of a quarter of a ball (A) and blend the seams. Build up the jaw with two disks, each made from a quarter of a ball (B). Blend the seams. Build up the profile with a flattened egg made of a quarter of a ball (C). Blend the seams and flatten the tip of the nose (D).

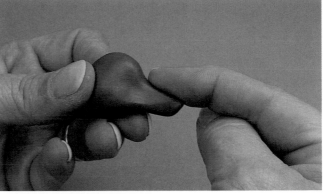

3 SHAPING THE MUZZLE

After pinching the sides of the muzzle, press down on the top with your finger to begin shaping the forehead. Finish by stroking the sides of the muzzle toward the head. This step will make the nose smaller and sharper and begin shaping the eye sockets.

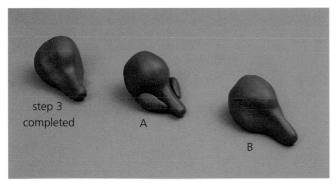

4 THE JOWLS

Apply two small, slightly flattened eggs to the sides of the muzzle (A), then blend the seams (B). Use ⅟₁₆ of a ball for each appliqué.

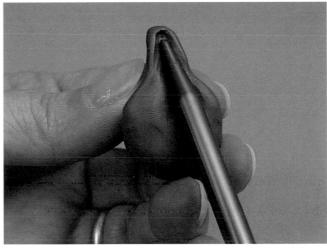

5 THE UPPER JAW

Press a large knitting needle into the clay on the bottom of the muzzle. Move it from side to side to form a triangular hollow for the upper jaw.

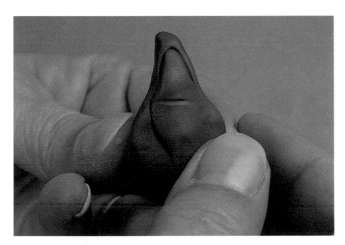

6 THE LOWER JAW

Form an elongated egg from ⅛ of a ball and flatten it slightly. Fit it into the upper jaw. Imagine or lightly mark a midline and blend the seams to that line.

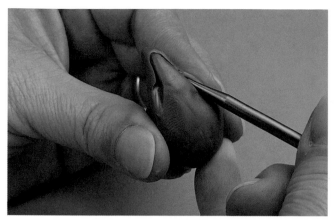

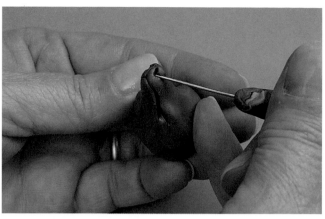

7 Accent the corners of the mouth with a medium knitting needle.

8 MARKING THE NOSE

The fox's nose is a smaller version of the basset hound's. Use the same techniques given on page 58. Begin by pressing diagonal grooves on the sides of the nose with a small knitting needle. Use a fine needle to split the lip. Mark the **U**-shaped nostrils with the fine needle, beginning with the inside of each **U**. Widen the inside of each **U** with a small tapestry needle.

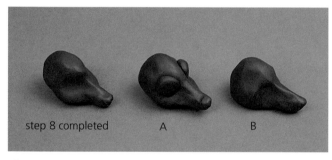

step 8 completed   A   B

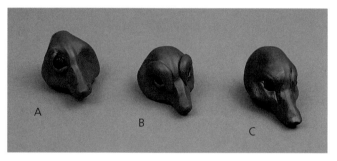

A   B   C

9 THE BROWS

Shape two disks, each from ¹⁄₁₆ of a ball, and place in the eye sockets (A). Blend the top seams first, building up the brow. Take care when blending onto the muzzle and jowls (B).

10 THE EYES AND LIDS

Position the eyeballs halfway between the tip of the nose and the back of the head. For each pair of eyelids, divide ¹⁄₁₆ of a ball into quarters. Use one of these quarters to shape a thin rod of clay for the lower lid. Wrap it around the base of the eye and trim off the extra clay (A). Use the remaining ¾ of a ball to shape the upper lid into a long, slightly flattened teardrop (B). Blend the seams using the tapered end of a knitting needle as a roller. Accent the corners of the eyes and brows and press a central groove in the forehead (C).

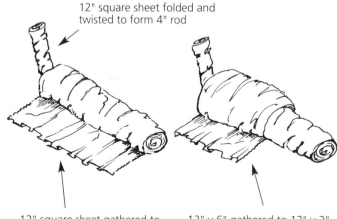

12" square sheet folded and twisted to form 4" rod

12" square sheet gathered to 12" × 3"

12" × 6" gathered to 12" × 2"

11 SHAPING THE BODY ARMATURE

The fox's body armature is a smaller version of the fawn's body armature. Use the same techniques, but smaller sheets of foil. Begin by folding a 12" (30.5cm) square sheet of foil in half. Gather, then twist tightly to form a cylinder 4" (10.2cm) long. Bend 1" (2.5cm) from one end to form the neck. Wrap the body with a 12" (30.5cm) square sheet of foil, gathered to 3" wide × 12" long (7.6cm × 30.5cm). Press or roll firmly to shape. Build up the ribcage and shoulder blades with a single 12" × 6" (30.5cm × 15.2cm) sheet of foil gathered to 12" × 2 (30.5cm × 5.1cm). Wrap tightly around the body near the neck and press firmly into shape.

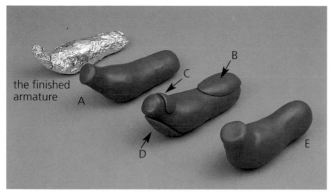

12 BUILDING UP THE BODY

Use three balls to plaster the body armature with small pieces. Rub smooth, then use three balls to make an oval pancake ⅛" (0.3cm) thick. Stretch and wrap around the body. Blend the seams and rub smooth (A). Apply an oval disk made of ¾ of a ball to the rump (B). Thicken the nape of the neck with an oval disk made of a quarter ball (C). Build up the chest and neck with an elongated oval disk made of a full ball (D). Blend the seams (E).

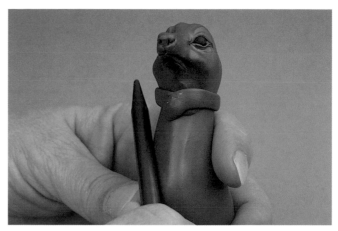

13 ATTACHING THE HEAD

Attach the head to the neck and secure with a collar made of ¼ of a ball of clay. Blend the seams.

14 BUILDING UP THE NECK

Build up the fur on the neck and ruff by applying two appliqués to each side of the neck. Made of a quarter ball each, these slightly flattened rods follow the contours of the neck. You may wish to apply and blend these appliqués one at a time.

15

Frame the face with a small, curved rod behind each eye. Use ⅛ of a ball for each rod and blend carefully.

16 THE EARS

Trace the ear pattern and construct two ears using the same techniques you used to fashion the bear's and fawn's ears (pages 52 and 70). Pierce a socket for each ear halfway between the eye and the back of the head. Pinch the base of the ear as you insert it. Secure with a rod of clay made from ¹⁄₁₆ of a ball. Wrap the rod completely around the base of the ear and blend the seams.

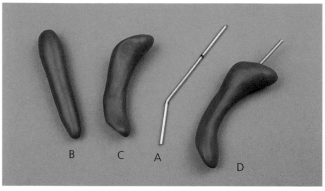

17 THE FRONT LEGS

Mark and bend a 2½" (6.4cm) armature rod according to the pattern diagram on page 78. Coat with vinyl glue and let dry (A). Shape ¾ of a ball into a 1¾" (4.5cm) long tapered rod (B). Flatten each end at an angle so the leg has a slight bow shape (C). Prepierce the leg at the stump end, then thread onto the armature rod. Stroke, stretch and wiggle the leg to ease it around the bend in the rod until the stump meets the top mark on the armature rod (D).

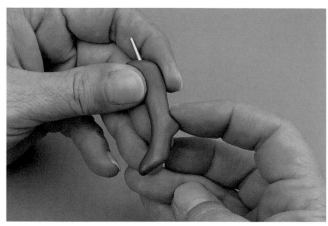

18 SHAPING THE FRONT LEG

Gently pinch the back of the lower leg just above the paw. Stroke from the paw upwards, first on the back of the leg, then the front and sides. The paw should reduce in size and the lower leg should become thinner. Use your fingers to refine the "heel" of the front foot by gently pinching the clay.

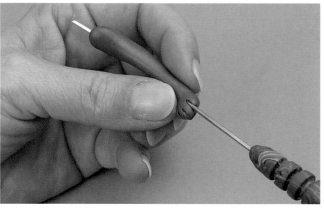

19 MARKING THE TOES

Mark four toes on each paw, using the same technique you used for the cottontail and the basset (pages 37–38 and 61–62). These are small paws with small toes, so use your small tools—the fine needle and the small tapestry needle.

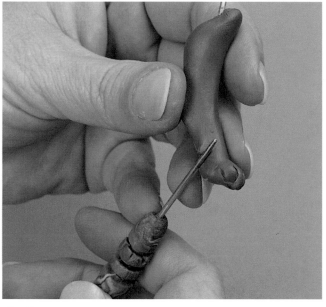

20 SHAPING THE DEW CLAW

Pinch the clay on the inside of the leg just above the paw to raise a tiny bump. A quick, light, downward stroke will finish the dew claw.

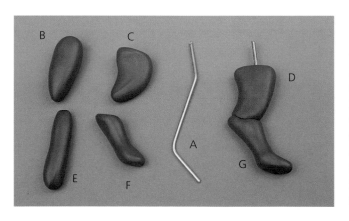

21 SHAPING THE HIND LEG

Follow the diagram on page 78 to mark and bend a 2¾" (7cm) armature rod. Coat the rod with glue and let dry (A). Roll ¾ of a ball into an elongated egg and flatten slightly (B). Curve this piece to form a "comma" shape (C). Flatten the stump and prepierce. Thread the thigh onto the bone (D). Stretch and stroke the clay so that it fits between the top and bottom marks. Let it rest while you shape half of a ball into a rod (E), slightly flattened at each end (F). Prepierce and thread onto the bone, stretching the clay until the two parts of the limb meet (G).

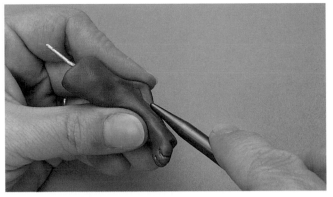

22 REFINING THE PAW ON THE HIND LEGS

Blend the seams, then refine the leg by stroking from the paw upward toward the heel. Pinch the heel, making it narrower, then draw a gentle groove just inside the heel and following its contours. Mark and define four toes on the paws. There is no dew claw on the hind foot.

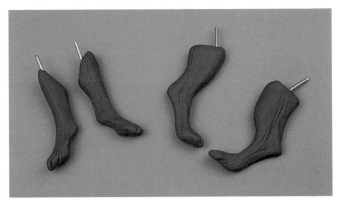

23 FINISHING THE LEGS

To ensure the fox will stand properly, hold each leg upright and press gently against the table. Texture each leg completely, then bake on an index card in a glass pan at 275° F for twenty minutes.

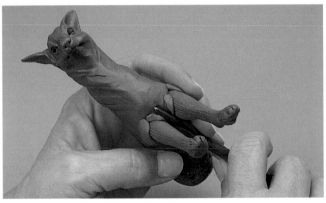

24 ATTACHING THE FRONT LEGS

Mark the center line, the shoulder, hip and quarter lines just as you did for the basset and the fawn (page 73). Pierce the body right into the foil core where the shoulder and hip lines cross the quarter lines. Insert and seat the front legs. Secure the inside seams with rods of clay each made of 1/16 of a ball of clay. Use a rod made from 1/8 of a ball to secure the outside of each front leg.

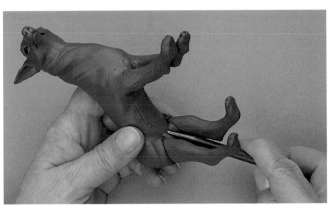

25 ATTACHING THE HIND LEGS

Insert and position the legs. Secure the inner seam with a rod made of 1/16 of a ball. Use a rod made of 1/8 of a ball on the outer seam.

26 THE SHOULDERS AND THIGHS

Form an oval disk from a half ball and position on the shoulder (A). Use an oval disk made from a full ball to build up the thigh (B). Blend the seams and finish shaping the shoulder with a knitting needle just as you did with the fawn (page 73).

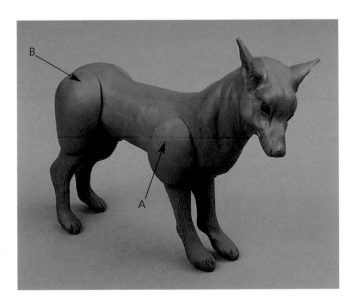

TIP

Your fox doesn't have to have all four feet on the ground to be stable. A three-legged stance is possible, even though his legs are prebaked. The thick layer of clay on the fox's body makes it possible for you to experiment with the pose, to move one leg forward or another back. Seating the left foreleg more deeply into the clay made this finished pose, the promise of a tentative step, possible.

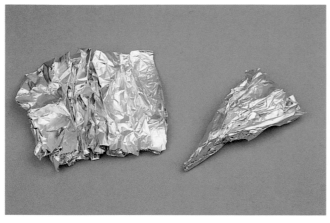

27 MAKING THE TAIL ARMATURE

Fold a 12" × 6" (30.5cm × 15.2cm) strip of foil, making it 3" × 12" (7.6cm × 30.5cm). Gather to 4" (10.2cm), then pinch the unfolded side. It should resemble a crumpled fan.

28

Hold the pinched end of the tail armature and crimp the opposite end. Press into shape by rolling it firmly against a table top. Pierce the base of the tail and insert a 1½" (3.8cm) rod. Use Super Glue to secure the wire.

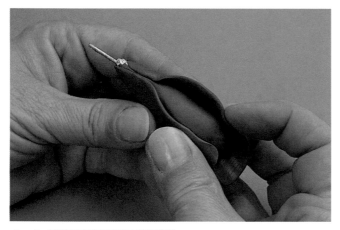

29 BUILDING UP THE TAIL

Cover the tail armature with 1½ balls of clay. Begin by pressing small pieces into the crevices, covering the armature. Roll the remaining clay into a sheet, wrap it around the tail, rub smooth and shape.

30 FINISHING THE TAIL

Bend the wire. Texture the tail completely, using a medium knitting needle to draw short, wavy lines, then add finer lines with a small tapestry needle. Bake for twenty minutes on parchment paper or an index card. When cool, pierce the rump and insert the tail. Secure by working clay from the rump onto the tail.

TEXTURE PATTERNS

TIP

How do you create fur that's both downy and detailed? Give the sculpture as much fine detail as possible. After baking, a vigorous but gentle scrubbing under hot water with a well worn scrubbing pad or a fine sanding pad will soften the hard edges and smooth out some of the texture. Take your time. Be selective and use a bright light.

31 TEXTURING AND BAKING THE RED FOX

Begin by drawing or pressing deep, wavy lines on the neck and shoulders with a large knitting needle. Vary the depth and length of your strokes. Finish the texture by drawing fine lines with a tapestry or small knitting needle. Work in those hard-to-reach areas first. Don't forget to texture the insides of the ears.

Bake the red fox with the same care you used to bake the fawn. Stand him upright for twenty minutes, then lay him on a thick cushion of cotton batting or folded paper towels. Place a soft but firm prop between his legs. Use a glass pan and bake for one hour at 275° F.

32 PAINTING THE WASH COATS

Apply several Burnt Umber washes over the entire animal. Paint the lower legs black with thin, staining washes. Let the paint dry between each coat to avoid streaking. Apply two or three Black washes until the legs are Black. Do the same to the insides of the ears.

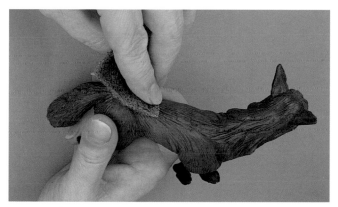

33
When dry, use a soft scrubbing pad to remove paint from the raised areas on the body, neck and head, but not the legs.

34 THE WHITE COAT

When the Black paint is dry, paint the belly, chest and neck, the lower jaw and jowls and the tip of the tail Titanium White. Use thin layers of paint, letting it dry between coats. Feather your strokes where the white and red fur meet, or use a dry brush technique and a small brush. Finish with a blend of Burnt Umber and Raw Sienna and a small brush to refine and soften the border fur.

35 THE LAST DETAILS

Paint the nose Black. Very carefully, paint a thin Black shadow around the eyes. Give the eyes a golden hue with a bit of Raw Sienna and let dry. The fox has a vertical, slightly oval pupil. Use the small brush for these tasks. When dry, varnish the eyes with gloss varnish.

The Bull Frog

I n early summer, male bull frogs gather at the pond's edge. Night after night, each frog sits on his own private stump or lily pad and sings of his superior position. The call of one such frog will make your ears tingle. The chorus of a dozen frogs is deafening.

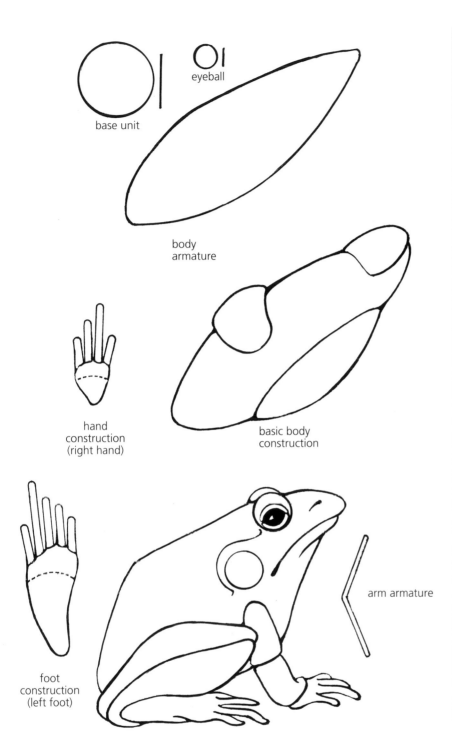

base unit

eyeball

body
armature

hand
construction
(right hand)

basic body
construction

foot
construction
(left foot)

arm armature

The frog's body begins with a tapered oval armature. Simple appliqués give the body its characteristic "froggy" shape. Stiff wire rods support the cylindrical front legs. Tapered rods form both parts of the hind legs and need no armature. The dotted lines on the hand and foot show the true length of the fingers and toes. Modeling the fingers and toes over beading wire and baking them helps them keep their shape. The bulbous eyes begin as prebaked eyeballs set into balls of clay. The distinctive ear comes from a stamp made of a rod of baked clay.

1 MEASURING THE CLAY

The frog's color is two parts Green, one part Raw Sienna and one part Ecru. You'll need one package of Green and half a package each of Sienna and Ecru. Divide the Green into eight sections. Divide each of the half packages of Raw Sienna and Ecru into eight sections. You will only need six sections of each color. Combine one section of each color together to make a ball of muted green clay 1⅛" (2.9cm) in diameter. Continue to combine to make six balls. Cut each ball in half and roll the halves into balls a little smaller than ⅞" (2.2cm) in diameter, the base unit for the bull frog. This project uses a little less than twelve balls of clay.

2 SHAPING THE ARMATURE

Fold a 12" (30.5cm) square sheet of foil into thirds, making it 12" × 4" (30.5cm × 10.2cm). Gather lengthwise and twist tightly to form a rod 3" to 4" (7.6cm to 10.2cm) long (A). Wrap the center of the rod with two 12" × 6" (30.5cm × 15.2cm) sheets, each gathered to 12" × 2" (30.5cm × 5.1cm) (B). Gather a 12" × 12" (30.5cm × 30.5cm) sheet to 12" × 3½" (30.5cm × 8.9cm) and wrap (C). Roll and press firmly against a table top (D).

3 Use a small hammer to flatten one end slightly to form a spatula shape for the mouth.

4 Turn the armature on its side and use the hammer to shape the hip sockets.

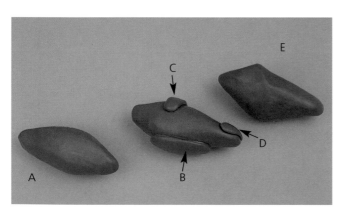

5 BUILDING UP THE BODY

Use one ball of clay to plaster the armature. Combine 1½ balls to make a flat oval sheet a little less than ⅛" (0.3cm) thick and wrap around the body. Use your fingers, then the palm of your hand to rub the clay smooth (A). Look at the frog's body from all sides to make certain it's well balanced. If you're uncertain, examine its reflection in a mirror. Apply a flattened egg made of ¾ of a ball to the center of the belly (B). Use a half ball to make a slightly flattened rod to build up the hips. Place this rod across the back at the hip line, ⅓ the distance from the tail (C). Apply a flattened oval made of a quarter ball to the top of the nose (D). Blend the hip appliqué first, then blend the belly, then the nose (E). Take care not to over blend.

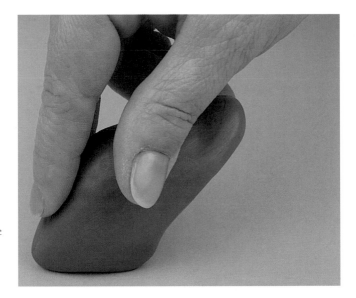

TIP
Creating a sculpture with smooth, symmetrical contours is one of the most difficult skills to master. Patience is the key, so take your time. If you find your fingers are leaving prints or depressions in the clay, stop! Let the clay rest and cool down a bit before you continue.

6 REFINING THE BODY
Press the rump against a flat surface. This will accent the **V**-shaped vertebra at the base of the spine and give the frog's back its distinctive shape.

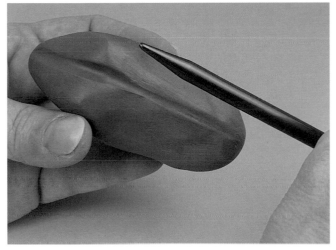

7 Use a large knitting needle to press a groove along the middle of the back. Rub your finger along the groove to give it a gentler shape.

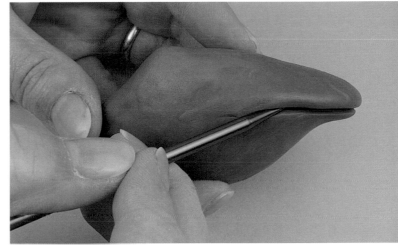

8 MARKING THE MOUTH
The frog's large mouth is ⅓ the length of the body. Mark the lip line by drawing the shaft of a small knitting needle through the clay, creating a deep groove.

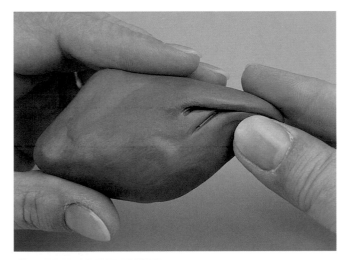

9 REFINING THE MOUTH
Accent the corners of the mouth with a large tapestry needle, then gently press the lips closed.

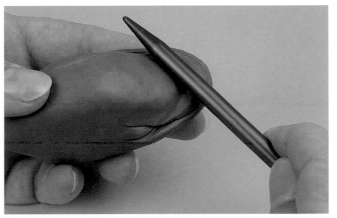

10 FINISHING THE LOWER LIP
Use the shaft of a large knitting needle to accent the lower lip.

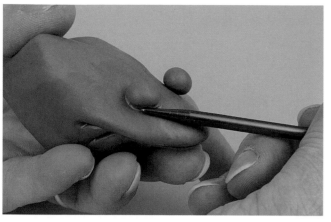

11 SHAPING THE EYELIDS

Use a ball of clay made from ¹⁄₁₆ of a ball for each eye. Position on an imaginary quarter line ¼ of the distance between the tip of the nose and the tail. Use the shaft of a large knitting needle to blend the seams all the way around.

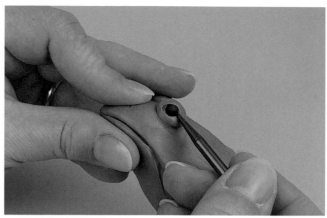

12 SETTING THE EYES

Use the rod method to measure a small amount of Black clay for eyeballs a little larger than ¼" (0.6cm) in diameter. Bake for twenty minutes at 275° F. Insert the eyeballs. Slowly and gently pat and press the eyelid clay against the eyeball. If necessary, use thin, ¼" (0.6cm) long rods of clay to finish shaping a smooth, oval lid.

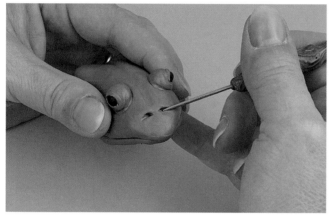

13 THE NOSE

Use the large tapestry needle to mark the nostrils halfway between the mouth and the eyes.

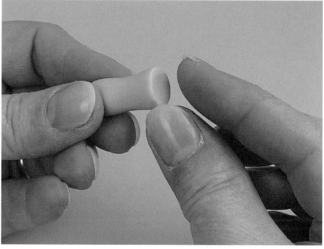

14 MAKING AN EAR STAMP

The easiest method for shaping the bull frog's large, round ears is to make an ear stamp. Use scrap clay to form a ½" (1.3cm) diameter rod. Press one end flat, then use your fingertip to press a slight hollow at the flat end of the rod. Turning the rod as you make this hollow will help the stamp keep its round shape.

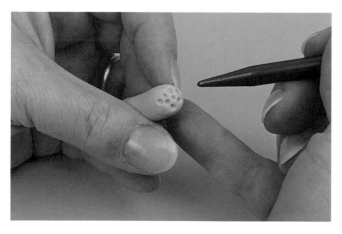

15 FINISHING THE STAMP

Use the point of the large knitting needle to press tiny dimples in the other end of the ear stamp. Adding these dimples gives the ear stamp a dual function: It is now also a perfect tool to create the bull frog's slightly warty texture. Stand the stamp upright in a glass pan and bake for thirty minutes at 275° F.

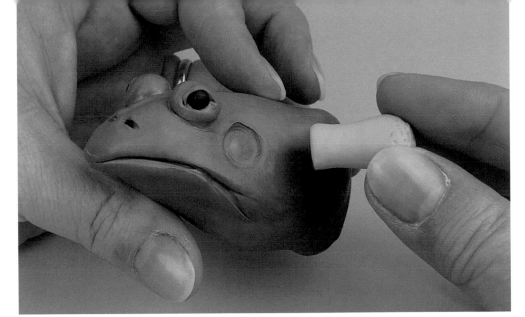

16 USING THE EAR STAMP

Dust the undimpled end of the ear stamp with corn starch (to keep the clay from sticking), then press it into the frog's body below and behind the eye. Gently spin the stamp as you press it in place.

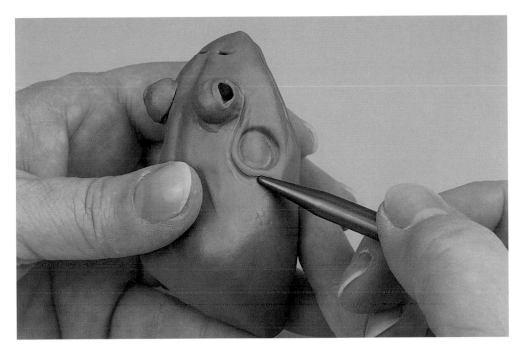

17 FINISHING THE EAR

A raised ring of tissue begins at the eye and wraps halfway around the bull frog's ear. Use a large knitting needle to draw this structure in the clay. Finish shaping the ring by rolling the shaft of the knitting needle away from the ridge and toward the body.

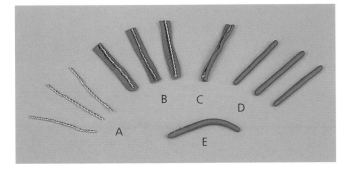

18 MAKING THE FINGERS AND TOES

Tightly twist together two 2' (61cm) strands of beading wire. Coat with vinyl glue and let dry. Cut the twisted strand into eighteen 1" (2.5cm) lengths (A). Roll half of a ball of clay into a very thin strip and cut this strip into strips as long as the armature wires and a little less than ¼" (0.6cm) wide. Press the armatures onto the clay strips (B). Fold the clay over the armature wire (C), pinch firmly, then roll gently between your fingers (D). Bake on card stock in a glass pan for twenty minutes at 275° F. When cool, carefully bend each finger and toe slightly (E).

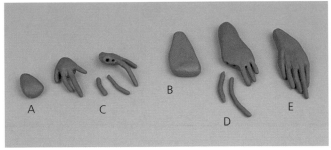

19 MAKING THE HANDS AND FEET

Follow the pattern guide on page 87 to cut the baked fingers and toes to the desired length. A nail clipper is the perfect tool for this task. Use ¹⁄₁₆ of a ball for each palm. Roll each ball to form an egg and flatten (A). Use half of a ball for each hind foot. Form the half ball into an extended egg and flatten (B). Refer to the pattern guide as you insert four fingers into each palm (C) and five toes into each foot (D), inserting each digit one at a time and blending the seams after each is inserted. Press the tapered end of a small knitting needle between each toe to suggest the webbing (E). You may need to reshape the hands and feet as you work.

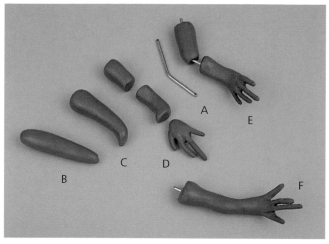

20 MAKING THE ARMS

Bend a 1¾" (4.5cm) long piece of stiff wire in the middle and treat with vinyl glue (A). For each arm, roll ⅜ of a ball (cut ¾ of a ball in half) into a slightly tapered rod (B). Flatten the large end and bend the small end to shape a wrist (C). Cut the arm in the center with a sharp blade (D). Attach the wrist to the hand and blend the seams. Pierce the upper arm and forearm, but not the hand, and thread onto the armature rod (E). Let the arm rest, then blend the seams at the elbow (F).

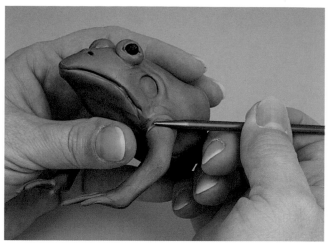

21 ATTACHING THE ARMS TO THE BODY

Attach the arms to the body at the shoulder lines just below the ears. Blend the seams by working clay from the arms onto the body. Strengthen and thicken the shoulder joint by placing a rod under each arm. Use 1/16 or less of a ball for this appliqué. Blend the seams, then place the frog in the proper sitting pose to finish setting the arms in place. Take care not to disturb the ears.

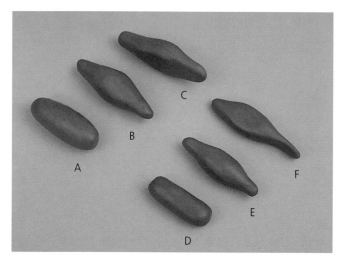

22 MAKING THE HIND LEGS

For each thigh, roll 1¼ balls into a 1½" (3.8cm) long rod (A). Taper each end to shape a 2" (5.1cm) long thigh (B). Finish by slightly flattening one end (C). For each calf, roll ¾ of a ball into a 1¼" (3.9cm) long rod (D). Taper each end to shape a 1¾" (4.5cm) long calf (E). Flatten the calf slightly. Pinch one end as shown, making the calf the same length as the thigh (F).

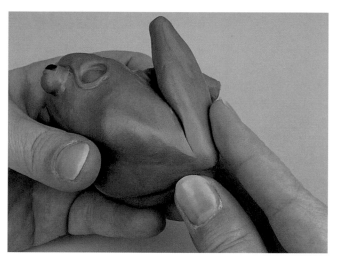

23 ATTACHING AND ASSEMBLING THE LEGS

Attach the thighs at the hips and blend the seams at the hip joint.

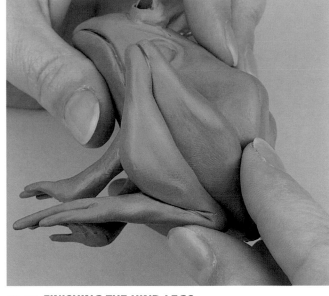

24 ATTACHING THE FOOT TO THE LOWER LEG
Wrap the pinched end of the lower leg around the heel and blend the seams.

25 FINISHING THE HIND LEGS
Press the lower leg into position against the thigh and blend the seams at the knee. Use your fingers to give the knee a slightly square shape. Finish by standing the frog upright and adjusting the position of the hind legs, if necessary.

TEXTURE PATTERNS
There are wrinkles and folds in the frog's skin, especially on the eyelids, around the arms and at the hip crease. The pebbled texture is random.

26 TEXTURING THE FROG
Use the shaft of a small knitting needle to press wrinkles and folds in the skin, especially at the shoulders and around the arms and legs. Use a large tapestry needle to press folds on the hands and eyelids. Use the dimpled side of the ear stamp tool to gently press warts here and there on the frog's body. How much texture is up to you, but use a light touch with this tool to avoid creating obvious depressions in the clay.

27 BAKING THE FROG

The frog's fingers and toes are delicate. Bake the frog standing upright for twenty minutes, then lay him on his back on a thick cushion of folded paper towels for the final forty minutes. Use a glass pan and bake at 275° F.

28 THE DRY BRUSH COAT

Use a medium or large bristle brush to apply a stippled, Titanium White dry brush coat on the belly and under jaw. Lightly tap the tips of bristles against the surface, beginning in the center of the belly and working outward. Finish this coat by applying a light dry brush to the entire frog and let dry.

29 PAINTING THE STAINING WASH

Mix Raw Umber, Permanent Green and Raw Sienna paint to form a transparent, golden-green staining wash. Use a soft brush to apply this wash to the entire frog. Before the coat dries, use a soft paper towel to blot some of the stain from the belly and lower jaw. Let dry.

30 PAINTING THE STRIPES AND SPOTS

The bull frog's markings range from an unadorned, green body (the most common) to a heavily spotted body. The legs usually have stripes. Use a medium or small soft brush to paint irregularly-shaped stripes on the frog's legs and arms. If you choose to give your frog spots, suggest a pattern. If you paint a spot on a hip or an eyelid, paint another spot (or two closely spaced, small spots) on the other hip or eyelid. Don't paint twin spots in exact corresponding positions, but do suggest a symmetry.

TIP

If the spots and stripes seem too bold, lighten them by applying a second green staining wash over the entire frog. Don't forget to blot the belly; it's always very light.

31 PAINTING THE LAST DETAILS

Darken the ear drum with a Raw Umber wash. Paint the eyeballs Black and let dry, then use a small brush to paint the iris with Gold. Take your time painting the iris; it will take two or three coats. When everything is dry, make the eyes shine with gloss varnish.

The Fledgling Bluebird

Within days of his first flight, the fledgling bluebird begins to shed the dull and downy camouflage of his youth. Slowly, brown flight and crown feathers are replaced by blue ones. By summer's end, his speckled breast takes on a rosy hue. This fledgling's feathers are a soft combination of blue and brown. Very soon, he will be on his own.

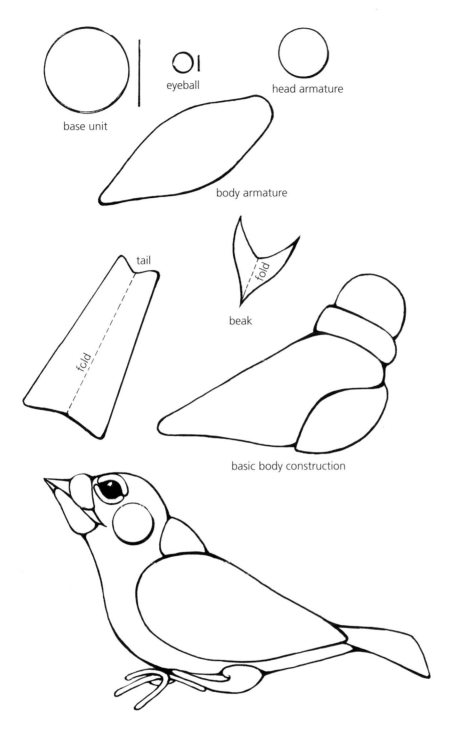

base unit

eyeball

head armature

body armature

tail

fold

fold

beak

fold

basic body construction

This little bird uses a body armature similar to the frog's and a round foil core in the head. Glue-sized card stock supports both the beak and the tail, while twisted beading wire strengthens the claws. Using a paper pattern makes marking the tail and wing feathers an easy task.

WHAT YOU'LL NEED FOR THIS PROJECT

Polymer Clay
- Cobalt Blue
- Ecru
- prebaked eyeballs made from Black clay, ³⁄₁₆" (0.5cm) in diameter

Armature
- 6" × 3" (15.2cm × 7.6cm) sheet of aluminum foil
- 12" × 5" (30.5cm × 12.7cm) sheet of aluminum foil
- three 12" × 6" (30.5cm × 15.2cm) sheets of aluminum foil
- 3" × 3" (7.6cm × 7.6cm) sheet of card stock stiffened with Super Glue
- beading wire

Tools
- blade for cutting the clay
- ruler
- fine needle tool
- small and large tapestry needle tools
- small, medium and large knitting needles
- wire nippers
- small hammer

Acrylic Paints
- Black
- Cobalt Blue Hue
- Raw Sienna
- Titanium White

Brushes
- no. 00 synthetic
- no. 1 and no. 3 round bristle brushes
- no. 6 synthetic round or filbert

Other Supplies
- paint mixing tray or four small jar lids
- paper towel for wiping dry brush
- vinyl glue (Sobo, Gem Tac or Aleene's Tacky)
- Tracing paper and hard pencil or fine-line pen (not a ball point)
- gloss varnish

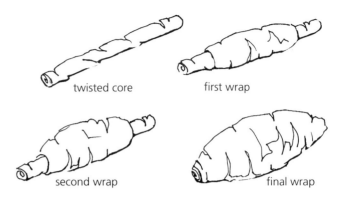

twisted core

first wrap

second wrap

final wrap

1 MEASURING THE CLAY

The bluebird's color is a blend of one part Cobalt Blue and four parts Ecru. You'll need a fourth of a package (one bar) of Cobalt Blue and one package of Ecru. Divide the bar of blue clay into four sections. Divide the package of Ecru into four bars. Combine one section of each color together to make a ball 1⅛" (2.9cm) in diameter. Continue to combine sections to make four balls. Cut each ball in half and roll into a ball ⅞" (2.2cm) in diameter, the base unit for the bluebird. This project uses less than six balls of clay.

2 SHAPING THE BODY ARMATURE

This is smaller version of the frog's body armature (page 87). The twisted center rod uses less foil, a 12" × 5" (30.5cm × 12.7cm) sheet folded to 12" × 2 ½" (30.5cm × 6.4cm). Gather lengthwise and twist tightly to form a foil rod 2¼" (XX cm) long. Wrap the center of the rod with two 12" × 6" (30.5cm × 15.2cm) sheets, each gathered to 12" × 1½" (30.5cm × 3.8cm). Gather a 12" × 6" (30.5cm × 15.2cm) sheet to 12" × 2½" (30.5cm × 6.4cm) and wrap around the rod, then roll firmly against a table top. Use a hammer to round the neck and flatten the tail. It should match the armature pattern on page 97.

3 BUILDING THE BLUE-BIRD'S BODY

Plaster the body armature with ¾ of a ball and rub smooth. Combine 1¼ balls and roll to form an oval sheet about ⅛" (0.3cm) thick and wrap around the body. Blend the seams and rub smooth (A). Build up the chest with an oval appliqué made of a half ball (B). Blend the seams (C).

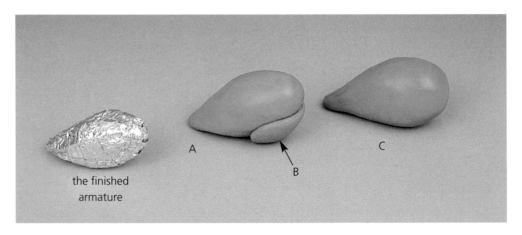

the finished armature

A

B

C

4 MODELING AND ATTACHING THE HEAD

Shape a ½" (1.3cm) diameter round foil core from a 6" × 3" (15.2cm × 7.6cm) sheet of foil, folded to 3" (7.6cm) square (A). Cover with half of a ball of clay (B) and attach to the body using a collar made of a quarter ball of clay (C). Build up the nape with an oval strip made of ⅛ of a ball (D). Blend the seams, then widen the jaw with two small disks, each made of ¹⁄₃₂ of a ball (E). Blend the seams (F).

C

D

A

B

E

F

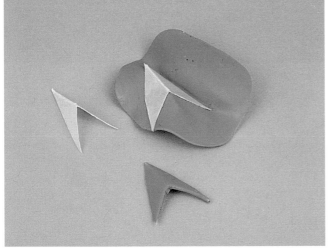

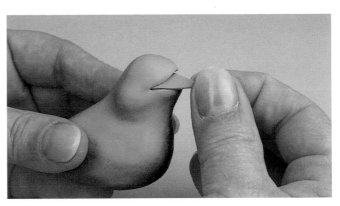

5 THE BEAK

Trace the beak pattern (page 97) onto a sheet of glue-sized paper or card stock. Cut and crease according to the pattern. Coat the armature with vinyl glue and let dry. Roll a very thin sheet of clay from 1/16 of a ball. Press onto the beak armature and trim the excess.

6 INSERTING THE BEAK ARMATURE

Pinch the beak as you firmly press it into the center front of the head.

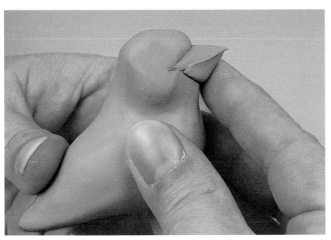

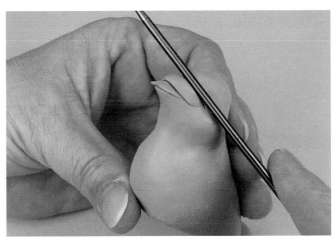

7 SHAPING THE LOWER BEAK

Form a cone from 1/32 of a ball and press into place below the beak armature. Blend the seams and refine its shape by working clay from this appliqué onto the neck.

8 SHAPING THE UPPER BEAK

Build up the upper beak with a small strip of clay made from a 1/32 of a ball. Blend the seams and refine the upper beak by working clay from the beak onto the face, then use a small knitting needle to define the beak's contour.

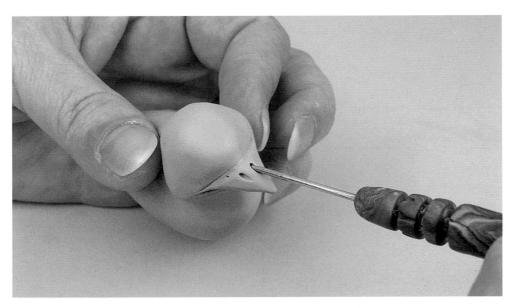

9 MARKING THE NOSTRILS

Mark the nostrils with a small tapestry needle.

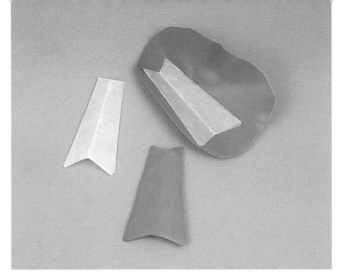

10 THE EYES

Make and bake a pair of Black eyeballs ³⁄₁₆" (0.5cm) in diameter. Place the eyes on the sides of the head one eye-width back from the beak, above the jaw.

Both eyelids can be formed from ¹⁄₃₂ of a ball of clay. Begin with the lower lids and use a knitting needle to place and secure small ¼" to ½" (0.6cm to 1.3cm) long rods of clay for each eyelid. After the eyes are finished, tilt and turn the head, if you wish.

11 MAKING THE TAIL

Trace the tail pattern from page 97 onto a sheet of card stock sized with Super Glue. Cut, then fold the tail armature lengthwise to shape it. Coat with a vinyl glue and let dry. Cover the armature with a thin sheet of clay and rub smooth. A quarter of a ball is more than enough clay to cover the armature.

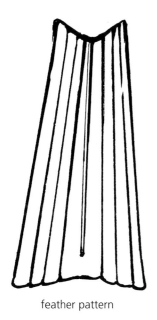

feather pattern

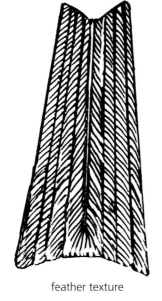

feather texture

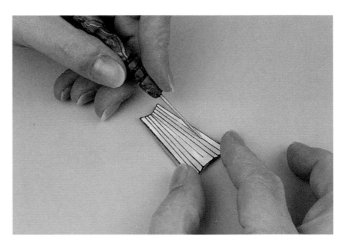

12 MARKING THE TAIL FEATHERS

Copy or trace the tail feather pattern at left onto a sheet of paper and cut out. Place the pattern on the clay-covered tail. Use a tapestry needle to trace along the pattern lines, drawing with enough pressure to emboss the pattern into the clay, but not so hard that you pierce the paper.

13 FINISHING THE TAIL

Remove the tail feather pattern and redraw the feather contours, making them sharper. Use a small tapestry needle to draw the fine barbules in the tail feathers. Following the feather texture pattern above, mark the outer feathers first, then the inner feathers. Bake the tail for twenty minutes at 275° F.

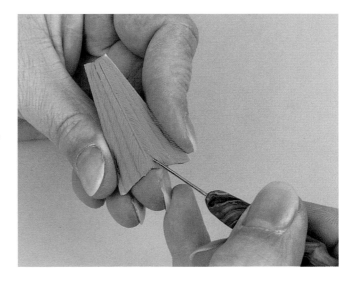

100

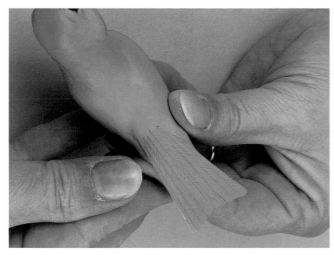

14 ATTACHING THE TAIL
Center the midpoint of the tail on the end of the body. Secure both the top and bottom of the tail by working clay from the body onto the tail.

wing pattern

15 MAKING THE WINGS
Use a half ball for each wing. Roll to form an extended egg, then press flat. The egg should be slightly larger than the wing pattern above. Copy or trace the wing pattern onto a sheet of paper and cut out. Place the pattern on the clay and trim the excess clay with a sharp blade. Trace the feather contours with a large tapestry needle, then remove the paper.

16 FINISHING THE WINGS
Enhance the feather contours with a large knitting needle. Use a bright light to insure you trace every contour, including the central quills of each feather. Finish the wing by removing burrs or loose clay scraps with a soft paint brush. Stroke from the top of the wing toward the wing tips. Let the wings rest a while before you attach them to the bird's body.

17 ATTACHING THE WINGS
Carefully and lightly position the wings on each side of the body. One wing tip should overlap the other wing tip. Use a fine needle to mark and trim the covered wing tip. Gently remove the covered wing tip and press the wings against the body.

18 SECURING THE WINGS

Use the shaft of a knitting needle to secure the wings at the shoulders. Redraw any smudged feather contours.

TIP

Drawing feathers is no more difficult than drawing fur. Practice on a small "egg" of clay to find the stroke and rhythm that is best for the way you work. If small burrs, or rough spots, occur it means you're drawing too deeply. Lighten your stroke by establishing a faster rhythm.

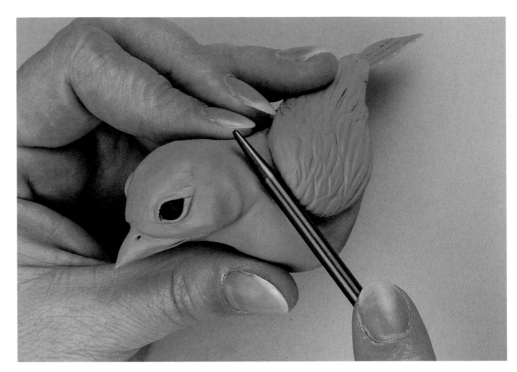

19 CREATING FEATHERS

Use a fine needle or the small tapestry needle and make light, short strokes. Follow the texture diagram and always begin with the central vein. Curve your strokes to define the feather's shape. Mark the feathers on the head and body before texturing the wings. Feathers overlap on the wings. Begin with the longer flight feathers and work your way up and back, toward the shoulders.

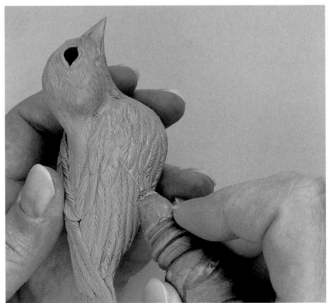

TEXTURE PATTERNS

Small oval feathers cover the head and body. They radiate away from the eyes and beak, growing toward the tail. Look closely and you'll see how the growth pattern resembles shingles on a scalloped roof.

mark the central vein

mark left side

mark right side

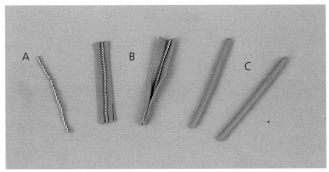

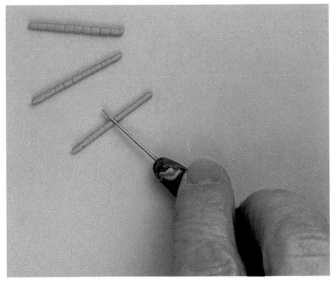

20 MAKING THE CLAWS

Twist together two strands of beading wire, enough to make a 4" (10.2cm) twisted strand. Cut into four 1" (2.5cm) long sections (A). Cover each with a thin strip of clay (B), then roll between your fingers until the wire is barely covered (C). The claws should be less than 1⁄16" (0.4cm) in diameter, thinner than the frog's fingers and toes. 1⁄16 of a ball is enough clay to cover all four claws.

21 TEXTURING THE CLAWS

Roll each clay-covered claw back and forth beneath a small tapestry needle to mark the scales.

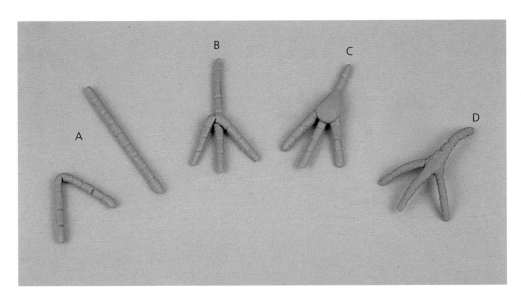

22 ASSEMBLING THE FEET

For each foot, fold one claw into a **V** (A) and center on a straight claw (B). Flatten a 1⁄8" (0.3cm) diameter ball of clay and use to secure the claws in place (C). Carefully rub the center of each foot smooth to seal the seams, but don't disturb the scales on the claws. Bake for twenty minutes. When cool, give each claw a slight downward curve (D).

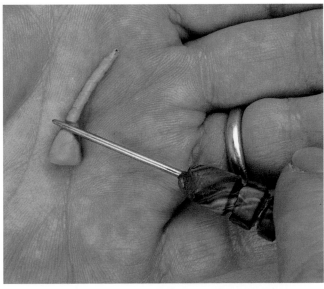

23 MAKING THE LEGS

For each leg, roll a 3⁄4" (1.9cm) long cone from 1⁄16 of a ball. Lay the leg in the palm of your hand and roll it back and forth beneath a small tapestry needle.

24 ATTACHING THE LEGS

Place the stump end of the leg on the bird's belly. Position the leg on the quarter lines (halfway between the center line and the outside), midway between the tip of the beak and the tip of the tail. Use a medium knitting needle to blend the seams and a small tapestry needle to texture. Bend the leg forward and gently press against the body.

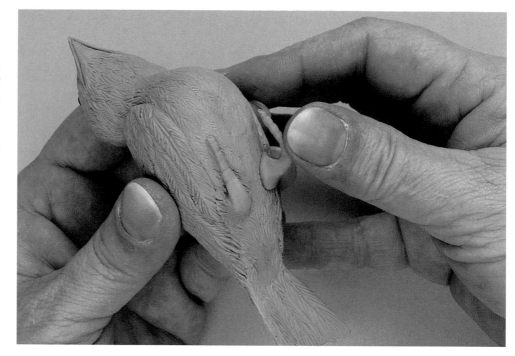

25 ATTACHING THE FEET

Press each foot into place on the "ankle" and carefully blend the seams with a small knitting needle, then bake the bluebird using the same time, temperature and technique used to bake the frog (page 94).

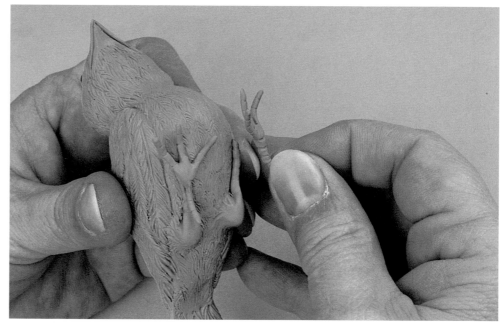

26 THE DRY BRUSH COAT

The fledgling bluebird is a warm, brownish-gray with a hint of blue. His breast is paler and speckled white. Begin with a soft white dry brush coat over the entire bird. Apply a second, light dry brush coat to the breast.

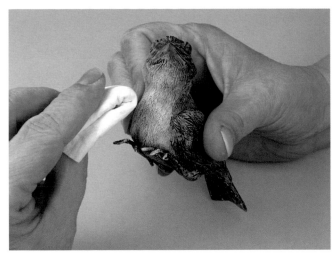

27 THE WASH COAT

Mix a wash of a Black, Raw Sienna and Cobalt Blue Hue. Stain the entire bird, using extra coats on the beak, legs and feet. Before the wash dries, blot the breast to remove some of the staining wash.

28

When the wash coat is dry, stain the edge of each wing and the tip of the tail Black.

29 THE DETAIL COAT

Paint small, white flecks on the breast. Use a small brush and a dry brush technique to paint white right around each eye.

Paint the eyes, the legs and feet Black. Finish by painting the tip of the beak Black. When everything is dry, give the beak, legs, feet and eyes a coat of gloss varnish.

TIP

Acrylic paints darken as they dry. If you've applied a staining wash and it seems too dark after it has dried, don't despair. You can easily lighten it with a second dry brush coat and restain with a lighter wash. This technique can produce greater depth as light interacts with the multiple layers of color.

The Siamese Kitten

I t is not known how the goblet vanished from the temple, only that it had. A brave and devout temple cat took it upon himself to find the treasure. "Harmony is gone," he told his wife, Dao, and she agreed. For endless days they scoured the jungle and found the cup at last. Dao lay down beside it. "Husband," she said, "fetch the priest and I will guard the goblet." With that, Dao curled her long body around the cup and wrapped her tail around the stem. When her husband returned, he found his wife nursing five newborn kittens, each with curiously kinked tails. When Dao released the cup at last, her tail possessed the same curious kink.

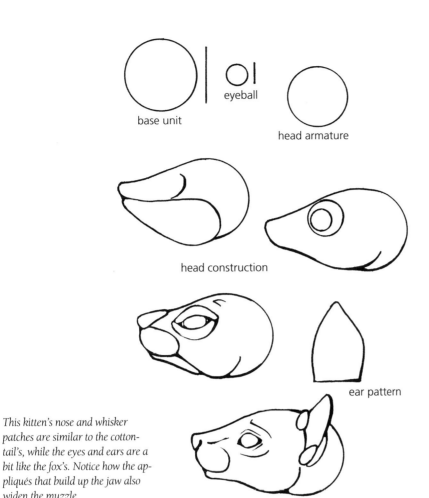

base unit

eyeball

head armature

head construction

ear pattern

This kitten's nose and whisker patches are similar to the cottontail's, while the eyes and ears are a bit like the fox's. Notice how the appliqués that build up the jaw also widen the muzzle.

WHAT YOU'LL NEED FOR THIS PROJECT

Polymer Clay
- Brown Granitex
- Ecru
- prebaked eyeballs made from light blue clay, a little larger than ³⁄₁₆" (0.5cm) in diameter

Armature
- 8" × 4" (20.3cm × 10.2cm) sheet of aluminum foil
- 12" (30.5cm) square sheet of aluminum foil
- 12" × 10" (30.5cm × 25.4cm) sheet of aluminum foil
- 12" × 6" (30.5cm × 15.2cm) sheet of aluminum foil
- card stock stiffened with Super Glue
- stiff metal rods
- heavy cotton string and beading wire

Tools
- blade for cutting the clay
- ruler
- fine needle tool
- small and large tapestry needle tools
- small, medium and large knitting needles
- wire nippers

Acrylic Paints
- Black
- Cerulean Blue
- Raw Sienna
- Raw Umber
- Titanium White

Brushes
- no. 00 synthetic
- no. 1 and no. 3 round bristle brushes
- no. 6 synthetic round or filbert

Other Supplies
- paint mixing tray or four small jar lids
- paper towel for wiping dry brush
- vinyl glue (Sobo, Gem Tac or Aleene's Tacky)
- gloss varnish

1 MEASURING THE CLAY

This clay is a blend of two parts Ecru and one part Brown Granitex. You'll need one two-ounce (56.7g) package of Ecru and a half package of Brown Granitex. Cut each color into eight sections. Combine one section of Ecru with one section of Granitex. Blend thoroughly and roll to form a ball. Continue to make eight balls. Cut each ball in half. This is the base unit, a ¾" (1.9cm) ball of clay. This project uses a little less than fourteen balls of clay.

TIP

Granitex's unique colors come from fine fibers in the clay. When you cut a ball of clay in half, you won't cut these fibers; they're too tiny. Your knife will push them to the bottom, creating a dark line at the base of the cut. Scrape along this line with your fingernail to remove it. Otherwise, you'll find dark lines that resemble small worms in your sculpture. Some fibers will stick to the blade; wipe it on a paper towel after each cut.

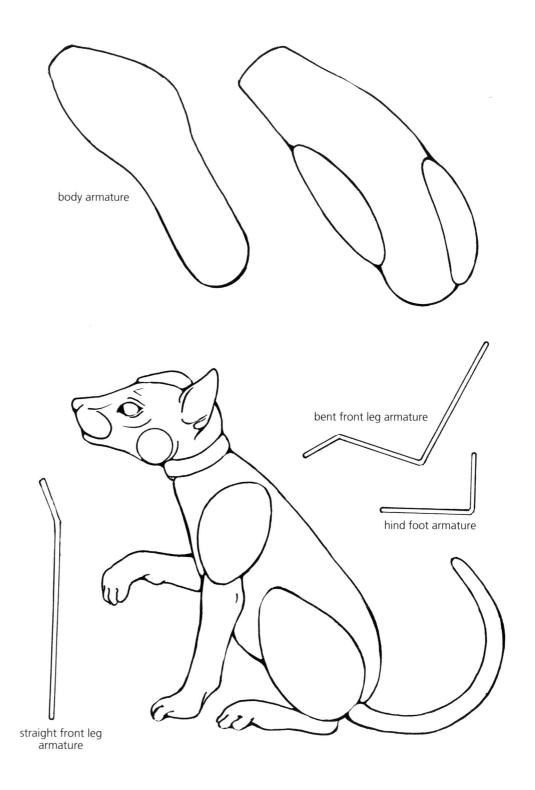

body armature

bent front leg armature

hind foot armature

straight front leg
armature

Simple appliqués build up the belly, rump, shoulders and thighs on this variation of the dog's body armature. Stiff metal bones help the legs and feet hold their shape as you model them. Heavy cotton string wrapped with beading wire provides a strong but flexible armature for the tail.

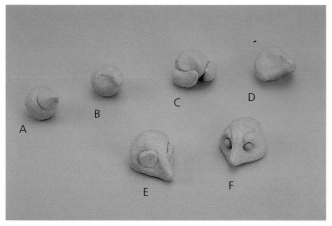

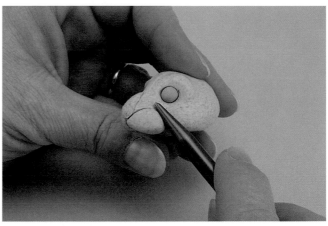

2 BUILDING THE BASIC HEAD

Use an 8" × 4" (20.3cm × 10.2cm) sheet of foil, folded to 4" × 4" (10.2cm × 10.2cm), to shape a round foil core. Wrap the core with half a ball of clay. Add a cone made of ⅛ of a ball (A) and blend the seams. Flatten the tip of the cone to begin shaping the muzzle. As you pinch, pressure from your thumb and finger should create hollows on each side of the muzzle. These will be the eye sockets. Stroke toward the tip of the nose to flatten the top of the muzzle (B). Build up the jaws and widen the muzzle with flattened eggs, each made from a quarter ball (C). Blend the seams (D). Begin forming the eye sockets with a disk made of 1/16 of a ball for each socket (E). Blend the seams. Use leftover bluebird clay (a mixture of 4 parts Ecru to 1 part Cobalt Blue) to make a pair of eyeballs a little larger than 3/16" (0.5cm) diameter. Bake the eyeballs. Insert the eyeballs one eye-width apart and 1½ eye-widths from the tip of the nose and the base of the jaw (F).

3 THE MUZZLE

Add a small, egg-shaped whisker patch to each side of the nose. Use ½ of a ball for each patch. Seen from the front, these appliqués do not extend beyond the center of the eyes. Seen from the side, they do not extend as far as the beginning of the eyes. Build up the nose and bridge with a tiny, flattened egg made from 1/64 of a ball. Using the tapered end of a large knitting needle as a small roller, gently blend the seams of the whisker patches and the nose.

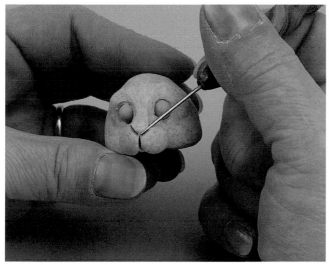

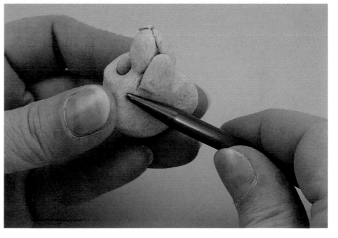

4 MARKING THE NOSE

Use the fine needle to mark a **Y** to split the upper lip and define the nose. Use a small tapestry needle to mark the nostrils.

5 MODELING THE MOUTH

Press the shaft of a knitting needle against the center base of the whisker patches, creating a hollow. Roll an egg from ⅛ of a ball and flatten slightly. Place on the lower jaw so that the small end of the egg forms the mouth. Blend the seams up to the whisker patches, then use the point of a small knitting needle to define the corners of the mouth.

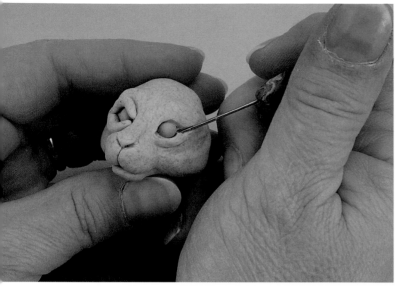

6 SHAPING THE LIDS

Use ½ of a ball to shape each lower lid and half that to shape each upper lid. Use the tapered end of a knitting needle as a roller to blend the seams. Use a small knitting needle or a large tapestry needle to draw the almond-shaped eye. Let the point of your needle rest on the eyeball and hold your tool at an angle so it gently scrapes against the lid to bevel it. You may have to repeat these steps to create the look you want.

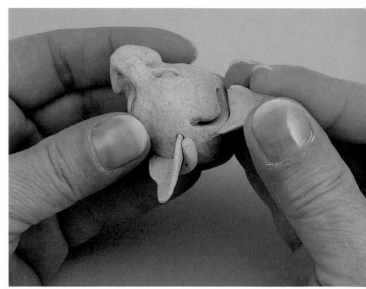

7 THE EARS

Trace the ear pattern (page 107) onto glue-stiffened card stock and cut out. Curl the armatures. Coat with vinyl glue and let dry. Use ⅟₁₆ of a ball to cover each armature with a thin sheet of clay. Trim off the excess clay and rub smooth. Place the ears in curved grooves in the head behind each eye, as far back from the eye as the eye is from the nose. Place a rod of clay made from ⅟₁₆ of a ball behind each ear. Blend the seams.

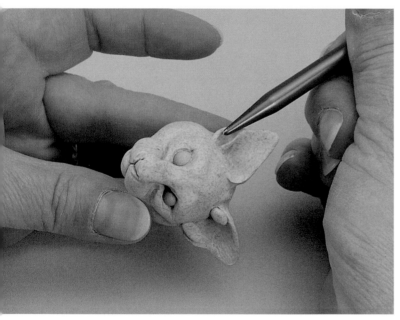

8 Place two tiny eggs of clay on each corner of the ear and blend the seams with a knitting needle. Suggest a fold in the outside corner of each ear by pressing with the tapered end of a knitting needle.

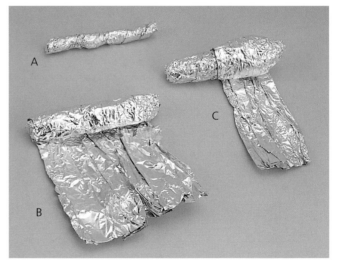

9 SHAPING THE BODY ARMATURE

Fold a 12" × 10" (30.5cm × 25.4cm) sheet to 12" × 5" (30.5cm × 12.7cm) wide. Gather and twist tightly to form a 3" (7.6cm) long rod (A). Wrap the rod with a single 12" (30.5cm) square sheet of foil, gathered to 3" wide × 12" long (7.6cm × 30.5cm) (B). Roll and press firmly to shape. Build up the ribcage and shoulder blades with a single 12" × 6" (30.5cm × 15.2cm) sheet of foil gathered to 12" × 2" (30.5cm × 5.1cm). Wrap tightly around one end (C) and press firmly into shape. It should match the armature diagram on page 108.

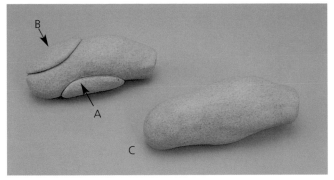

10 BUILDING UP THE BODY

Cover the body armature with two balls of clay. Use one ball for the plaster layer and one for the wrapping layer. Build up the belly with a flattened egg made of a full ball (A). Build up the lower back with a flattened egg, also made of a full ball (B). Blend the seams (C).

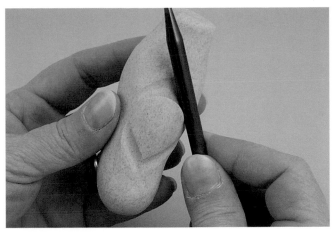

11

Use the shaft of a large knitting needle to press a **V** at the base of the belly and a gentle, upside down **U** above the belly. Rub with your finger to soften these grooves.

12 ATTACHING THE HEAD

Attach the head to the neck and secure with a collar made of ⅛ of a ball of clay. As you blend the seams, work some of the clay down onto the chest and shoulders.

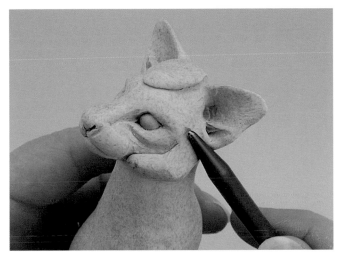

13 BUILDING UP THE JOWLS AND CROWN

Round out each jaw with a flattened egg made of ⅛ of a ball and blend the seams. Build up the crown with a small oval made of 1/16 of a ball

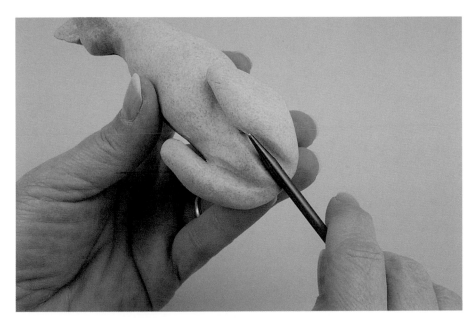

14 THE HIND LEGS

For each hind leg, form an egg from 1½ balls and flatten slightly. The large end of the egg should be flatter than the small end. The small end of the egg is the knee and should be slightly pointed. Place the egg at the side of the body, near the rump. Blend the seams at the base of the thigh, where the thigh meets the rump, and at the loins.

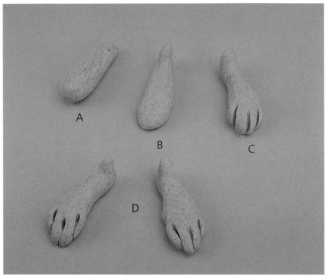

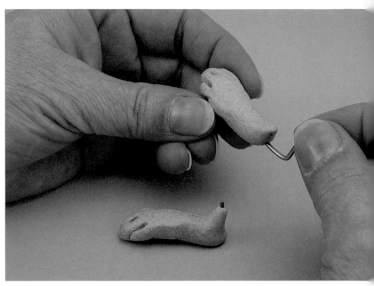

15 **THE HIND FEET**
For each hind foot, form an extended egg from a half ball and flatten slightly (A). Curve the feet to form a right and left foot and bend the heel to form an ankle (B). Mark four toes with a small tapestry needle (C). Define the outer toes by pressing a small knitting needle against the sides of each foot. Widen the cleft between each toe with the tip of a knitting needle (D).

16 Insert the **L**-shaped foot armature into each heel and re-shape the ankle.

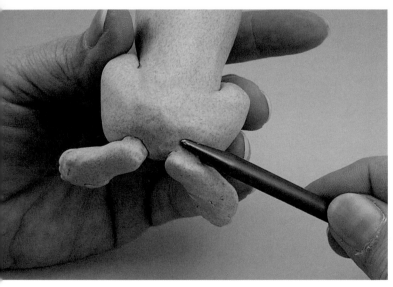

17 **ATTACHING THE HIND FEET**
Use a small knitting needle to make a socket at the base of the hind leg and insert the ankle. Use a knitting needle to blend the seams at the ankle and define the heel.

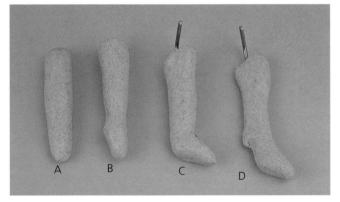

18 **THE STRAIGHT FRONT LEG**
Mark and bend the armature rod according to the pattern diagram on page 108. Coat with a vinyl glue and let dry. Shape a full ball into 1¾" long (4.5cm) tapered rod (A). Roll the small end between your fingers to shape a club (B). Flatten the club slightly and bend to form the paw. Prepierce the leg at the stump end. Thread onto the armature rod until the stump meets the top mark on the armature rod (C). Stroke from the paw upwards, first on the back of the leg, then the front and sides. Gently pinch the back of the leg just above the paw. Push up with the shaft of a knitting needle to refine the "heel" (carpal pad), just as you did with the fox's front leg on page 82 (D).

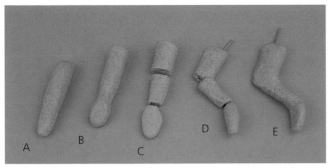

19 THE BENT LEG

The bent leg uses the same amount of clay as the straight leg. Start with a rod (A). Form a club and flatten the handle slightly (B). Cut the leg into three equal sections (C). One by one, pierce and carefully thread onto an armature rod marked and bent according to the pattern diagram on page 108 (D). Blend the seams, taking care not to lose the shape of the leg. Pinch the back of the leg just above the paw. Push up with the shaft of a knitting needle to refine the "heel" (E).

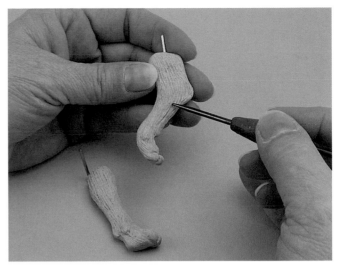

20 FINISHING THE FRONT LEGS

Mark four toes on each paw, using the same technique you used for the fox (page 82). Pinch the clay on the inside of each leg just above the paw to raise a tiny bump. A quick, light, downward stroke will finish the "thumb." Flatten the upper part of each leg slightly. Texture each leg completely. Bake for twenty minutes on a sheet of card stock in a glass pan at 275° F. When the legs are cool, bend the exposed armature rod according to the diagram.

21 ATTACHING THE FRONT LEGS

Mark only the center line, the shoulder and the quarter lines. Pierce the body into the foil core where the shoulder lines cross the quarter lines. Beginning with the support leg, insert and seat the front legs. Secure each leg with the shoulder clay, a flattened egg made of ⅛ of a ball.

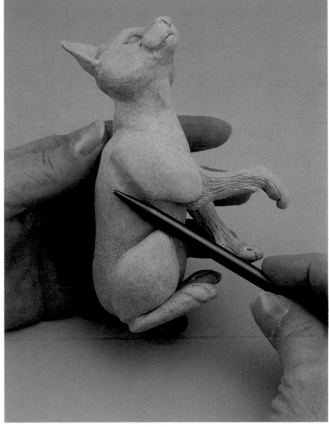

22

Press into place and blend the seams. Finish by using the shaft of a large knitting needle to model the shoulder blades.

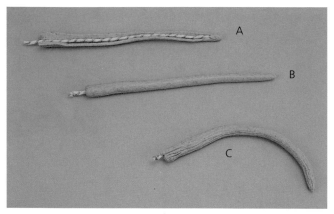

23 THE TAIL

Twist beading wire around a 5" (12.7cm) length of thick cotton string. Coat with vinyl glue and let dry (A). Roll a 4½" (11.4cm) long tapered rod from a half ball. Flatten and fold around the tail armature. Roll between your fingers, pinching slightly to seal the seam (B). Texture completely with a small tapestry needle (C).

TEXTURE PATTERNS

24 ATTACHING THE TAIL

Use a medium knitting needle to pierce the rump. Insert the tail. Carefully pose the tail and redraw any smudged texture.

25 TEXTURING THE SIAMESE KITTEN

Begin in those hard-to-reach areas: the belly, chest and neck. If necessary, gently move the feet aside so you can texture them. Hold the kitten by the shoulders or hind legs as you work. Texture those areas last. If the clay becomes soft from the heat of your hands, let it rest and cool for a while before beginning again. Bake the kitten sitting upright in a glass pan for twenty minutes at 275° F. After twenty minutes, lay the kitten on a cushion of folded paper towels and bake another twenty minutes. Take care how you lay him down to protect the tail and the ears.

26 PAINTING THE SIAMESE

The ears, feet and tail are very dark, especially on the edges of the ears, the paws and the tip of the tail. There is also a dark mask on the face. Begin with a Raw Umber wash on the kitten and let dry. Use a damp, clean, soft scrubbing pad to remove stain from all but the legs and feet, ears, tail and mask. Let dry, then use a soft brush to slowly build up the Raw Umber stain on the ears, mask, feet and tail. A dry brush technique will help you feather the edges. Take care not to get any paint on the eyes. Darken the paws, the edges of the ears and the tip of the tail with a wash of Raw Umber blended with a little Black. Use the same wash to darken the nose and outline the eyes. If necessary, use a blend of Cerulean Blue and White to brighten the eyes. Paint a vertical oval pupil in each eye, using a blend of Cerulean Blue tinted with Black and let dry. Darken the inside of the pupil with Black. Varnish the eyes with gloss varnish when the paint is dry.

TIP

If you find you're having trouble achieving a soft edge between the darker and lighter fur, blend Titanium White paint with Raw Umber and Raw Sienna to make a color matching the lighter fur. Use a soft brush and the dry brush technique to soften these areas.

CHAPTER FIVE

Changing the Size, Pose, Setting or Finish

Making Your Animals Smaller or Larger

The scale of a sculpture is its size compared to the objects it represents. The mouse, the bull frog and the bluebird are all life size, modeled on a one to one scale—1" (2.5cm) of sculpture equals 1" (2.5cm) of real animal. The other sculptures are smaller than life size and each has a different scale. For example, the black bear is ½ scale; each inch (2.5cm) of the sculpture represents a foot (30.5cm) of the real animal's size. The red fox is ⅙ scale, with 2" (5.1cm) representing every foot (30.5cm). That's every foot of height, width and depth. Change those dimensions equally and you change a sculpture's size and its scale.

Changing the size of a sculpture begins by changing the size of the base unit. However, it's not as simple as adding another equally-sized ball of clay to the base unit, because you've only doubled one of its three dimensions. (See the bull frog on the next page for an example of what happens when you simply double the base unit.) To make a sculpture twice as big in all dimensions as the original, you need to double the height, the width and the depth of the original base unit. Two times the height, two times the width and two times the depth equals eight balls of clay.

To think of it another way, if you double a recipe for cookies, you add twice as much of each ingredient. You wouldn't add twice as much sugar without adding twice the flour and twice the butter, right? The height, width and depth of the object are its ingredients, and each needs to be increased equally to make double the recipe.

The same holds true for making miniatures. You need to reduce all three dimensions: half the height times half the width times half the depth, or ⅛ of a ball of clay.

Changing the size and the pose of an animal, placing the animal in a setting or altering the finish can affect the mood of a sculpture. Combine these changes and new possibilities emerge.

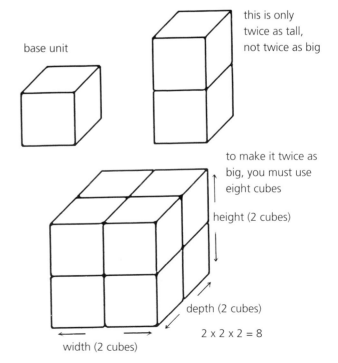

base unit

this is only twice as tall, not twice as big

to make it twice as big, you must use eight cubes

height (2 cubes)

depth (2 cubes)

2 x 2 x 2 = 8

width (2 cubes)

To change the scale of a three-dimensional object, you must change its height, width and depth equally. Imagine the base unit is a cube. Adding another cube of equal size may seem to double the size of the cube, but really you are only making it twice as tall (or wide or deep). Instead, you must double each dimension of the cube to make the object twice as big in all dimensions. Therefore, you will need to combine eight cubes to make a cube that is twice as big. The balls you use for base units in your sculptures also have height, width and depth, so to make them twice as big, you must double all three dimensions.

Scaling the Armature

Making miniatures means using thinner wire bones, glue-sized paper instead of card stock and smaller foil cores. Surprisingly, you don't use ⅛ the amount of foil to make a core that's half the original size. You use half the amount. Remember, it's the dimensions that matter—the length, width and depth. A foil sheet has a length, width and depth, but the depth—the thickness of the sheet—is minimal, small enough to not affect the overall dimensions of a foil core. Reducing the length and width to the proper size and a few taps with a hammer will do the job.

To create smaller foil cores, follow the same steps given in the project to form the cores, but reduce the size of each sheet by multiplying the desired scale by the length and the width. Don't simply cut the sheet in half, a temptation when making smaller round foil cores. This will cut only one of the dimensions in half. You need to reduce both dimensions. A 12" × 6" (30.5cm × 15.2cm) sheet of foil, folded in half, will make a ⅞" (2.2cm) round foil core, but a 6" × 6" (15.2cm × 15.2cm) sheet will make a core a little less than 8/10 the size of the original. You need a 6" × 3" (15.2cm × 7.6cm) sheet of foil, folded in half, to make a round core that's 7/16" (1cm), half the size of ⅞" (2.2cm). Whatever the size of the core, always multiply the desired scale by the length and width.

Creating larger sculptures means using stronger, thicker wire bones and larger foil cores. When forming larger foil cores the depth of the sheet does matter: use the wider, heavier foil. It will prove easier to enlarge and only slightly more difficult to gather and wrap. A little work with the hammer will do the rest.

Replacing the Foil Core With Clay

For very small, compact miniatures like the rabbit and seal, replacing the core with clay is often the best method for modeling. The original cottontail's head armature is equal to half the base unit. Combine that with the half ball used to cover the core and model the head. The body armature is equal to two balls of clay. Combine those two balls with the two balls of clay used to cover the core, then model the body. The seal's head is equal to half of a ball and the body equal to three balls. So use one ball to begin shaping the head, and four and a half balls to form the seal's body.

Adjusting the Baking Time

If you've changed the size of a sculpture or replaced the foil core with clay, adjust the baking time. Bake twenty minutes for every ¼" (0.6cm) thickness of clay. For larger sculptures with longer baking times, there's a risk of scorched ears, tails, fingers and toes. After twenty minutes, insulate the vulnerable parts of a sculpture by wrapping them with two or three layers of paper toweling, then cover this insulation with a small piece of aluminum foil, shiny side out, to reflect the heat.

TIP

Use a photocopier or a scanner and computer to reduce or enlarge the original pattern diagram to the desired size. From determining the size of the base unit and the eyeballs to constructing armatures and appliques, you'll have a ready reference. Use the rod method to measure the clay. To construct the right sized foil core, multiply the length and width of the foil sheets by the desired dimension. Then follow the original steps for construction.

The bigger bull frog, made by doubling the amount of clay and foil, is only twenty percent larger than the original. To make him twice as big as the original, I would have needed eight times as much clay and two times as much foil.

Both of these miniatures are half the size of their originals. To make these tiny animals, follow the same steps you used to make the originals. You'll still need ten balls of clay to make the cottontail and a little less than ten balls to make the seal, but you'll need only ⅛ the amount of clay and ¼ the amount of foil.

Changing the Pose

By changing the pose you can place two or more animals together. Whether the change you want to make is simple or more complex, the clay ratios—the amount of clay you used to make the body parts and appliqués—remains the same. Sometimes, you'll find that new armatures are necessary to support the new pose or that an appliqué should be shaped slightly differently.

Use what you've learned. Borrow the techniques you used in one sculpture to change another. Lower or raise an animal's head, bend or straighten a limb, open or close the eyes.... Small changes can make a big difference, and most of them are surprisingly simple. These animals illustrate changes you already know how to do. The clay ratios remain the same.

Opening the Bluebird's Mouth

Opening the bluebird's mouth means using an armature to strengthen the lower beak.

To open the bluebird's beak, follow these steps: Make and insert the upper beak, but don't fill it with a cone of clay to model the lower beak. Instead, use your finger to support the base as you model the top of the upper beak, including the nostrils. Divide the original fill clay in half, using one half to cover the lower beak. Insert the lower beak and use the remaining fill clay to secure it to the body. The mouth will close during this step; gently pry it open. If you wish, make a tiny tongue out a small strip of clay and press in place with a knitting needle.

"Flipping" an Animal's Pose

Both of these animals have similar poses. Both poses were made by turning the head around and treating the back as the belly, a technique I call "flipping."

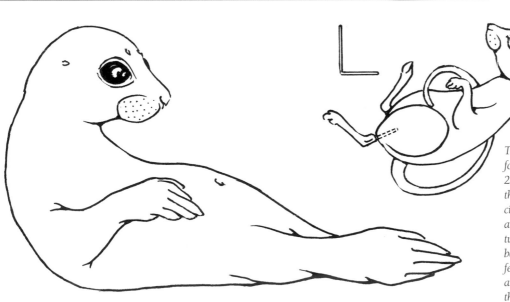

Only three changes are necessary to place the seal on his back. Follow the steps beginning on page 41 , but make three changes. Turn the head around. Make the flippers as usual, but reverse their position; this step places the "thumb" in the proper position. Last, dimple the navel.

To make the sleepy mouse above, follow the steps beginning on page 23, but make these changes. Close the mouse's eyes with small half circles of clay. Arch the body more and put the head on backwards, turning that arched back into the belly. When you model the hind feet, bend the heel to create an ankle and use an L-shaped armature in the feet. Remember, mice have five toes. Attach the arms after you attach the tail. Don't prebake the tail or you'll have difficulty placing it against the body.

Making a Dozing Fawn

To make this dozing fawn, give the body a gentle curve by bending the armature in the middle. Curve the neck armature as well, and don't use an armature rod when you attach the head. Take care not to stretch the neck when you blend the seam.

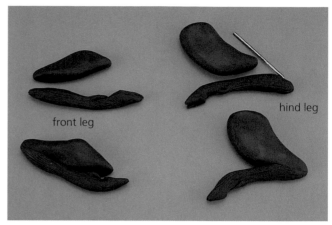

1 MODELING THE FAWN'S LEGS
To model the legs, follow the steps beginning on page 68, but make these changes: for the hind leg, mark a joint on the armature just above the hind claw position and bend down. Thread the lower leg onto the bones, model, texture and bake, then shape the upper leg. Note that there's no extra armature extending from the upper hind leg. It's not necessary for this compact pose. The front leg is easier to sculpt if you cut the armature at the "knee" and model each part of the leg separately. Model, texture and bake the lower leg before attaching the upper leg. Using no bones in the upper leg makes this a very easy attachment.

2 ATTACHING THE FAWN'S LEGS
Attach the legs at the hip and shoulders and secure with the thigh and shoulder clay. Attach the legs in pairs, beginning with the front leg. It is folded next to the body.

3 ATTACHING THE OUTSIDE HIND LEG
Place one hind leg so that it lies under the body. If necessary, curve the upper bone slightly to conform to the body.

Making a Standing Basset

There is a wire-wrapped string in the basset's tail, a technique borrowed from the cat. His hind legs use the same amount of clay as the seated basset, but some of that clay is in the thigh appliqué. You'll have to have to use a bit of that clay to shape the upper leg and you'll need bones in those legs.

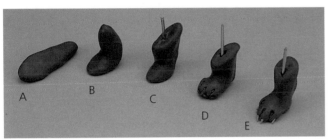

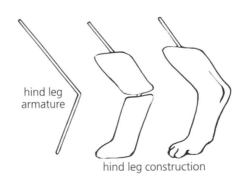

1 SHAPING THE STANDING HIND LEG

To make a standing hind leg, use the same amount of clay you used to make the hind foot, ¾ of a ball. Shape the hind foot (A), then bend to form the lower leg (B). Insert an armature rod ½" (1.3cm) longer than the leg. Pinch the back of the leg and stroke upward from the base of the foot, forming the base of the heel (C). Mark and define the toes (D), prepierce the toes and insert the claws (E).

2 ATTACHING THE HIND LEG

Pierce the body where the quarter and hip lines cross and attach the legs to the body. Blend the seams on the inside of the leg and attach the thigh. Notice how the thigh clay has a slight comma shape and curves back to finish the heel. When you blend the seams, the basset's hind leg will have the right shape. Use a large knitting needle to define a gentle groove at the heel just as you did for the fox's leg (page 83).

Making a Standing Siamese

Like the basset, you'll use the same amount of clay to change a sitting leg to a standing leg. Unlike the basset, the kitten's thinner legs mean bending the armature—a technique borrowed from the fox. Notice the kitten's back is straight and the tail hangs down.

hind leg armature

hind leg construction

To shape the kitten's hind leg, reduce the thigh clay to one ball, using the leftover half ball to shape the upper hind leg, and ¾ of a ball for the lower leg. Follow the modeling instructions you used to shape the fox's hind leg and attach it to the body in the same way. (Enlarge this drawing by 150% to use with the pattern on page 108.)

Now that you know how to change the size and pose, you can create family groups. Both the fox and basset pups are two thirds the size of their mothers. Because they are pups, I used a slightly larger eyeball, ¾ the original size, not ⅔. Note how the fox pup's paw is lifted, a technique borrowed from the cat.

Adding a Setting

If your carefully modeled and painted sculptures seem out of place, give them a habitat of their own. Creating environments begins with a roughly-textured slab of clay. Adding small rocks of marbled clay, sisal fiber shrubbery or blades of paper grass will deepen the illusion. Hobby and craft shops offer a wellspring of dried flowers and grasses that can lead you into a new world: habitat sculpture. The pictures at the beginning of each project are an example of this sculptural form.

MOSSY GROUND

Create mossy ground cover by pressing small pieces of green clay (bull frog green is perfect) onto the base. Use a knitting needle to add a realistic texturing by gouging jagged, interlocking spirals and swirls in the "moss" and the base clay.

BROAD GRASS

To make grass, use an archival paper close to the color of the grass—green for fresh grass, brown or yellow for dry grass. Paint both sides with a soft green or dull brown, using the thickness of the paint and parallel brush-strokes to simulate the grain of grass. When dry, cut the paper with the grain. Scale the blades of grass to suit the sculpture and plant grass in pre-drilled holes filled with glue. Incidentally, the large, broad-leafed plants used on the bull frog's base (top right) came from this same sheet of paper.

Whether it's a bit of mossy covered ground, a piece of the frozen North or a slab of stone from a swamp, the world you create should suit the animal. How much clay is enough? If the sculpture is standing on two legs, like the mouse, use half the amount of clay that you used to make the sculpture. If the animal stands on all fours or reclines, use at least the same amount of clay that you used to make your sculpture. Press with crumpled foil to create an earthy texture. Use tightly wadded foil to fill large rocks, using half as much clay as you would need to shape the rock entirely out of clay.

WHAT YOU'LL NEED FOR THE BASES

Polymer Clay
- Earth colors (Black, Raw Sienna, Ecru, Burnt Umber or blends of these colors)
- muted greens such as the bull frog green
- Granitex for rocks

Armature
- aluminum foil
- green, yellow or brown archival paper
- sisal twine

Tools
- scissors
- blade
- small and large tapestry needle tools
- small and medium knitting needles
- landscaping tool (page 10)

Acrylic Paints
- Black
- Burnt Umber
- Raw Sienna
- Raw Umber
- Sap Green
- Titanium White

Brushes
- no. 00 synthetic
- no. 1 and no. 3 round bristle brushes
- no. 6 synthetic round or filbert

Other Supplies
- paint mixing tray or four small jar lids
- paper towel for wiping dry brush
- cyanoacrylate glue (Super Glue)
- vinyl glue (Sobo, Gem Tac or Aleene's Tacky)
- PVC cement
- crumpled aluminum foil

FINE GRASS

To make finer grasses or reedy shrubs, unravel sisal twine and tint with acrylic paint mixed with varnish (for sizing). When dry, plant these grasses in the unbaked base with the forked end of the landscape tool. Place several strands between the tines and push the fork into the unbaked, textured clay.

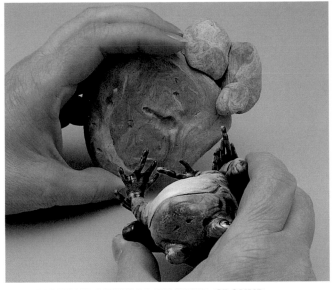

PUTTING YOUR ANIMALS ON SOLID GROUND

Press down gently to mark the footprints in the clay, making certain the animal is well seated. Dusting the feet with cornstarch will prevent the clay from sticking. With the animal in place, poke holes for grass blades or shrubs. Remove the animal, then bake the base for forty minutes at 275° F. When the base is cool, reposition the animal and secure with Super Glue, an epoxy glue or PVC clear cement (available at hardware stores). When securing the animal, make certain that the bottoms of the animal's feet are unpainted and free of corn starch to insure a strong bond.

The lightly washed rocks show the true color of this base, a blend of scraps left over from the seal, the cat and the white rabbit. Burnt Umber and Black staining washes, the same colors I used to paint the fox's fur, brought harmony to this piece. Slivers of paper grass provided just enough contrast.

MAPLE LEAF PATTERN

Enlarge at 133 percent to return to full size.

A LEAF BASE

If it hadn't been winter when I made this sculpture, I would have simply pressed a maple leaf onto a thin sheet of clay. Since no leaves were available, the paper embossing method used to mark the bluebird's wings worked just as well. A wire armature strengthened the clay-covered stem attached to the bottom of the leaf. Baking the leaf in a ring of cotton batting helped keep its shape. A Raw Umber wash enhanced the veins. Acrylic satin varnish gave the leaf a soft sheen.

Changing the Finish

It is possible to imitate the look of porcelain, marble, jade and ivory with polymer clay. This faux technique is inspired by the work of Tory Hughs, who first explored the possibility of simulating precious minerals with polymer clay. These techniques take full advantage of the color of the clay. The bronze bears use another technique, tinted mica powders, to achieve the look of metal. Changing the finish will change your sculpture completely.

BRONZE BEARS

Except for the finish, these two sculptures are identical. To achieve the metallic look, brush Brilliant Gold Pearl-Ex Powder, which contains tinted mica flakes, onto the unbaked clay. You'll find it easier to tint and bake the bears before attaching them to the base. Make the base and attach the bears by pressing their feet into the unbaked clay. Be sure there's no powder on the bottoms of their feet when you do attach them. Brush mica powder on the base and bake again for about forty minutes. After baking, apply a thin coat of acrylic satin varnish to the mica finish and let dry. Apply a Black wash to enhance the texture, followed by a final coat of satin varnish, tinted with Raw Umber.

PORCELAIN RABBIT

Two parts of White blended with one part Translucent Premo clay will create the same translucent look of Cernit White clay. You'll find this clay mixture easier to control than Cernit. Use the rod method to measure the clay (page 14). Create a broader, more sculpted texture with the large knitting needle. Use pink clay for the eyeballs made from four parts White to one part Red. After baking, a gentle sanding will make the white clay look like porcelain paste and will soften the texture. Use a dark pink to paint the pupil. Apply pale pink washes on the nose and ears. A glossy varnish on the eyes, nose and inner ears are the last details.

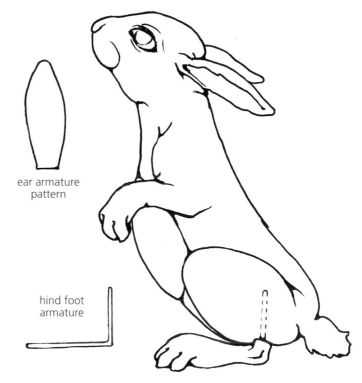

ear armature pattern

hind foot armature

*Don't be fooled by the white rabbit's pose. It's identical to the mouse's. Follow the steps you used to make the sleeping cottontail, but make a few changes. Use the same amount of clay you used to make the closed eye, but roll that clay into rods for the eyelids. Bend the body armature to arch the back. Form a disk from a full ball and place it on the center of the belly, omitting the belly fat on the sides of the body. Shape each hind foot, then bend the heel to form an ankle and insert an **L**-shaped armature rod. The ankle bones should pierce the body armature when you insert them. Make the front legs as usual, but bend the wrist. Use glue-sized paper armature to support the ears.*

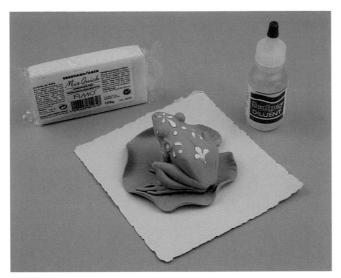

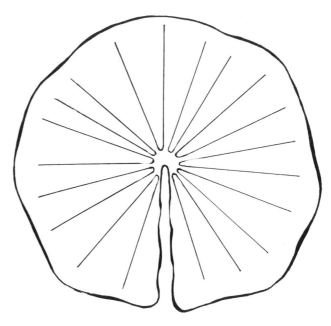

WEDGWOOD FROG

Combine one part of the blue used for the bluebird with four parts White to create the light blue for this Wedgwood frog. Use the rod method to measure the clay. Bake the frog first to insure he sits comfortably on the lily pad, then bake the lily pad. The white appliqués are simple shapes applied to a baked and lightly sanded frog. Rubbing Sculpey Diluent or a small lump of FIMO Mix Quick on the baked frog's back prior to adding the appliqués ensures that the appliqués will stay put. Bake the appliquéd frog for twenty minutes.

To make the lily pad , combine two to three balls of clay and roll to ⅛" (0.3cm) thickness. Use this pattern and cut out the pad. Use a knitting needle to draw light lines from the center of the leaf outward. Gently pinch and curl the edge of pad, then bake. When cool, use Super Glue, epoxy glue or clear PVC cement to secure the frog to the lily pad.

NETSUKE SEAL

This tiny seal, half the size of the original, is a netsuke: a bead or fastener made of simulated ivory. Ivory has a well-defined grain, so always make more than you need. To create ivory, use Ecru and Transparent clay. Roll each into rods. Lay side by side and roll again to make a single rod. Cut the rod in half and lay the two halves side by side so that the stripes of color alternate. Roll smooth again, repeating the same process ten to twelve times. Use the rod method to measure the clay. Take care to preserve the grain. Follow the same technique described for working with marble on the next page: Cut only what you need and flatten the slices into squares. Bake, wet sand and buff. Age the ivory with a wash of Burnt Umber, then buff again.

JADE RABBIT

This jade rabbit, 1½ times larger than the original, has shape but no texture. Combine one part of the green used for the bull frog with twenty parts Translucent clay to create this type of jade. Use the rod method to measure the clay. After baking, thorough sanding with fine-grade wet sandpaper and a superfine wet sanding pad made him very smooth. A wash of Raw Umber in the folds gave him the look of old jade, and buffing with an old denim scrap made him shine.

TIP

To make a true netsuke bead, replace the foil core with clay (page 117). Before baking, use a tapestry needle to carefully pierce a hole just below the armpits or through the length of the body. Widen the hole with a small knitting needle. Work the needle from both sides for a clean hole. Thread on leather or rattail.

MARBLE BIRD

Like the jade rabbit, this marble bird has almost no texture, only contour lines on the wings and tail. Turning the head and closing the eyes seemed a proper choice for this piece, as did the thicker tail. He has no feet or legs—another choice that seemed to fit this sculpture—and rests on a small, flat octagonal base made of the same marbled clay. Use thin semi-circles to close the eyes. Double the amount of clay to cover the tail. After baking, wet sand, then buff the marble to make it shine.

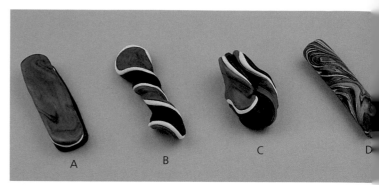

1 CREATING MARBLE

Stack three or four colors (A). Twist the stack twice (B), then fold in half (C). Compress, twist and fold two more times, then roll the clay to form a smooth rod the same diameter as the base unit (D). When making marble, always make more than you need; some of it will be lost as you work to preserve the pattern.

2 PRESERVING THE MARBLE PATTERN

Use the rod method to measure the clay. To preserve the pattern, mark the rod and cut the clay as you need it, but don't roll the cut sections into balls. Instead, press the slices as flat as the original appliqués. The flattened slices should be square. When cutting your flattened slices, cut into squares for round or egg shapes, rectangles for oval shapes and triangles for extended egg shapes, such as the wings. Fold the corners of the geometric shapes under into the right shape for the appliqué. For the wings, you'll need to stretch the clay. Use this method for all of the appliqués, even the very small ones, always working to preserve the grain in the marble pattern.

3 When you attach the head to the body, work to match the grain of the marble. Blend carefully using a large knitting needle as a roller.

TIP

To cover the marble bird's foil core, you'll need to use the single wrap method described on page 36. This means combining the clay for the plastering and wrapping steps. To do this, cut a single slice equal to two base units in length, then flatten, stretch and shape. The armature must be smooth, well formed and treated with vinyl glue for the single wrap method to work.

Resources

Books

My studio walls are covered with drawings and photographs of animals, all the result of research done at the library, in bookstores and on-line. My own personal art library has also grown. These are the books I find most helpful:

A Handbook of Anatomy for Art Students, Arthur Thompson. New York: Dover Publications, 1964. Understanding begins with ourselves. The thorough text on human anatomy makes similar books on animal anatomy easier to understand.

An Atlas of Animal Anatomy for Artists, W. Ellenberger, H. Dittrich and H. Baum. New York: Dover Publications, 1956. Annotated plates illustrating the skeletal, musculature and surface anatomy of fourteen animals, including the dog, cat, hare, deer and seal.

Drawing Animals, Norman Adams and Joe Singer. New York: Watson-Guptill Publications, 1979. Beautiful renderings, form drawings and anatomical studies, including bears, rabbits, cats, dogs and deer.

Drawing and Painting Animals (First Steps Series), Bill Tilton. Cincinnati, Ohio: North Light Books, 1997. Very useful, lively form drawings and lovely renderings presented as a course in drawing animals, complete with a final exam.

Die Gestalt des Tieres, Gottfried Bammes. Leipzig: Seemann, VEB, 1975. In any language, this book is a feast. The English language version, *The Artist's Guide to Animal Anatomy: An Illustrated Reference to Drawing Animals,* though still in print, is hard to obtain.

The New Clay: Techniques and Approaches to Jewelry Making, Nan Roche. Rockville, Maryland: Flower Valley Press, 1991. Though there is very little information about sculpting, there is a wealth of information about polymer clay techniques. This is the polymer clay bible.

How to Make Clay Characters, Maureen Carlson. Cincinnati, Ohio: North Light Books, 1997. Featuring projects of sweet simplicity, presented with care, this book is full of blending techniques for clays without the "smudge factor."

The Art of Polymer Clay: Designs and Techniques for Creating Jewelry, Pottery, and Decorative Artwork, Donna Kato. New York: Watson-Guptil Publications, 1997. Innovative techniques, beautifully presented—this book will inspire you.

Suppliers

Most art and craft stores sell polymer clay, but they may not have the brand or color you need. Most hobby and model shops sell miniature habitat materials and brass rods, but what you want may not be in stock. Here's a list of catalogue mail-order and internet suppliers of clay, tools and other materials:

Clay Factory of Escondido, Inc.
P.O. Box 460598
Escondido, California 92029-1030
Phone: (760) 741-3242; Website: www.clayfactoryinc.com
A source for Pearl-Ex Powders, Premo, Super Sculpey, Sculpey III, Liquid Sculpey, tools and tips.

Craft Woods
2101 Greenspring Drive
Timonium, Maryland 21093
Phone: (800) 468-7070; Website: www.craftwoods.com
A source for the wildlife wood carver, Craft Woods offers books and videos about wildlife art, model making supplies, sculpting tools, Super Sculpey, acrylic paints, brass rods and diorama supplies. Their catalogue is filled with tips on painting.

Micro-Mark
340 Snyder Avenue
Berkeley Heights, New Jersey 07922-1595
Phone: (800) 225-1066; Website: www.micromark.com
A mail-order source for the finescale modeler, Micro-Mark offers brass rods and small-scale sculpting tools.

The Polyform Products Company
1901 Estes Avenue
Elk Grove Village, Illinois 60007
Phone: (847) 427-0020; Website: www.sculpey.com
The manufacturers of my favorite clay, Premo, Polyform offers bulk sales of their clays. Their Website offers a gallery of polymer clay art, including my own, and a tips page that is second to none. You can also find out what stores in your area sell the clays you need.

Prairie Craft Company
P.O. Box 209
Florissant, Colorado 80816-0209
Phone: (800) 779-0615; Website: www.prairiecraft.com
A source for Premo, Super Sculpey, Sculpey III, Liquid Sculpey, Flexiclay, FIMO and FIMO Soft; also books, videos, tools and tips for the polymer clay artist.

Wee Folk Creations
18476 Natchez Ave.
Prior Lake, Minnesota 55372
Phone: (800) WEE-FOLK; Website: www.weefolk.com
A source for Premo, Super Sculpey, Sculpey III, Flexiclay, Cernit, FIMO and FIMO Soft; also books, videos, tools, metallic powders and list of classes taught by Maureen Carlson.

The Wildlife Artist Supply Company (WASCO)
P.O. Box 967
Monroe, Georgia 30655
Phone: (800) 334-8012; Website: www.taxidermy.com
A source for taxidermy artists, WASCO offers excellent books on animal anatomy and sculpting supplies. The free catalogue, always in demand, is well worth the wait.

Index